DATE DUE			
JUL 1 6 2010			

COMPLETE GUIDE TO FISHING

Building your own Rod

BO WESSMAN

COMPLETE GUIDE TO FISHING

Building your own Rod

MASON CREST PUBLISHERS, INC.

COMPLETE GUIDE TO FISHING – **Building your own Rod**
has been originated, produced and designed by
AB Nordbok, Gothenburg, Sweden.

Publisher
Gunnar Stenmar

Editorial chief
Anders Walberg

Design, setting & photowork:
Reproman AB, Gothenburg, Sweden

Translator:
Steven Hill

Nordbok would like to express sincere thanks to all
persons and companies who have contributed in
different ways to the production of this book.

World copyright © 2003
Nordbok International,
P.O.Box 7095,
SE-402 32 Gothenburg, Sweden.

Published in the United States by
Mason Crest Publishers, Inc.
370 Reed Road, Broomall, PA 19008
(866) MCP-BOOK (toll free)
www.masoncrest.com

First printing
1 2 3 4 5 6 7 8 9 10
Library of Congress Cataloging-in-Publication Data on file at
the Library of Congress

ISBN 1-59084-550-1

Printed and bound in the Hashemite Kingdom of Jordan

Contents

# Preface

Even a beginner's first hand-built rod can – and will – be better than the products that are sold by stores. The explanation lies in the fact that one builds for oneself, which enables the work to be done with the precision one wants in all handicraft, and allows adaptation of the product for the user and purpose to a degree that no mass-manufactured rod can attain. The result is usually a rod that has better performance and quality than its commercial counterparts.

To achieve such a result, the rod-builder must do a little more than assembling a kit. Building rods from ready-made kits is not at all recommended – instead one chooses the materials and composes a rod that meets one's own requirements and desires. If one then independently designs the handle and reel seat, and places these and the rod guides on the rod in a manner that best exploits the rod blade's properties, one has a tool that functions optimally. And finally, if one carries out the assembly work as exactly as is possible in this kind of handicraft, the rod becomes a maximally durable and robust piece of equipment.

Why build your own fishing rod?

The other day I heard a comment about the fishing rod crafting course I am going to hold at the fishing club this autumn. It was one of the older members, a man who has probably not acquired new fishing tackle for the last 20 years, and whose rod is now so patched up and repaired that it is's completely unrecognizable. I have even seen him rooting through old rod parts of entirely different makes and types to replace a broken top tip on a £2030 dollar rod. Anything that has a top ring and bends is apparently good enough! This man cried out overWhen he heard about the newly advertised fishing rod crafting course he cried out : "Build a fishing rod, is it really worth it?"

The answer is obvious. Of course not! He quite clearly considers that fishing tackle should not cost money, and that anything whatsoever will do the job. So the truth of the matter in his case is unfortunately already decided, I cannot't teach him anything he could derive any benefit from. And even if he is naturally welcome on my course, I do notn't think he would get anything out of it.

Even if this gentleman's view of the matter is somewhat extreme, the truth is that when most people try their hand at building a fishing rod for the first time, they do so to save money. By mounting the components yourself you can cut down on the workmanship costs and get the the longed for fishing rod you cannot actually afford a little cheaper. A hand-crafted -made rod is often seen as a slightly inferior copy of a factory-made one, and the fact that in spite of this you hope it will not be too much worse than a rod from the shop, overweighs the difference in price.

The idea of a cheap "home-made" fishing rod fails, however, to live up very well to reality, for several reasons. The assembly costs are nowadays such a small part of the sales price that there is hardly any difference with between a finished rod if you buy all the parts separately. With all the work that has to be put in, and if you share the widely held misunderstanding that hand-made fishing rods are not just not as good as fishing rods from the factory, well once again the answer is clear. It i's not worth building fishing rods! When the presumptiveprospective builder builders of a fishing rod discovers this then perhaps their interest will dwindle away, which would be a pity, because building building fishing rods is enormously rewarding in completely many different ways.

Another side of the same coin is that as a builder crafter of

fishing rods I often have to explain for to my potential customers why the fishing rods that I have built made are not cheaper than the mass produced equivalents in the shop. Once again there is the same misunderstanding, that a "home-made" rod is an inferior copy of the one from the factory and that the only motivation for their existence is that they are cheaper. In actual fact the truth is quite the reverse, a hand-made rod is far superior to all the "cheap" fishing rods you can find in a shop.

I once divided up a 14 foot spinning spinning rod into a four-sectioned rod for a customer. There were no suitable four-sectioned rods to be bought, so I sawed off a finished two-sectioneds rod and constructed twoo new tubes ferrules so that it becameto make it four-sectioned. There was no problem in doingdoing this and the rod was delivered in good order. A week later the telephone rang – the rod had broken in the tubeferrule!

The concept of "custom" means individual adaptation and highest possible quality, often combined with a special and costly design.

the rod in the holder and non-stretch braided line on the reel, I could see, even more satisfied, that my "home-made" tubes ferrules had withstood this direct maltreatment without problem, while the "factory tubeferrule" had not.

To end the matter I repaired the broken tube ferrule so that it had the same construction as the others, in return for payment of course, and since then he has not had any problems. I did, by the way, inform him that he ought to use some other method of getting his hook loose from the bottom in future.

It i's easier now to get people to believe that the fishing rods I build, and I have been doing it a while now, are of better quality than the ones you buy in the shop, rather than that the same applies to all hand-made crafted rods. But in actual fact a beginner's first rod will, if it is built be with due care and if he follows certain basic principles and procedures when building it, which are not at all difficult to learn, understand or apply, be considerably better than any "cheap" fishing rod from a factory somewhere. This applies both to the quality – a hand-made rod lasts longer – and the performance. A hand-made rod will functions better, and, throws cast further and with better precision, and so on, than a factory- built rod. And this is, what my stingy club mate will never understand or appreciate, the real motive for building your own fishing rods.

Better rods

This book will teach you how to build fishing rods, and I would like to emphasis from the very beginning that it has nothing whatsoever to do with assembling building kits. It is about crafting creatively, designing yourself, regardless of prototypes, your own fishing rod, with the blank and the other components as raw materials. You will of course also learn how to assemble building kits, but crafting fishing rods only becomes a rewarding hobby when you start to "Custom" your own rod.

Building fishing rods should be governed by the fishing conditions and by the user's (you yourself) way of fishing and personal requirements. The result will be a personified rod that will not resemble the rods you are used to, but which is adapted to you and your way of fishing. You will then be rewarded, seldom with monetary gain, but with sensitivity, comfort, qual-

There was no good reason for one of my tubes ferrules to break during normal use and I strongly suspected an attempt to "fiddle" the guarantee, that the tube ferrule had been clenched or broken by force somehow and the owner wanted to try to get me to take responsibility for the damage because of itsin view of it incorrect construction. In the car on my way to the customer I even began to get somewhat quite angry annoyed and prepared myself for a rather agitated conversation. To tell the truth by the time I arrived I was quite charged uppretty angry.

So then I saw the rod and could, both disappointedly foolishly and admittedly rather pleased, confirm that it was the middle tube ferrule that had broken, i.e. the one that had been on the rod before I modified it. My fit of anger vanished and when I heard what had happened, that the person in question had got their hook stuck on the bottom when trolling and tried to run loose the spoon with the boat, with

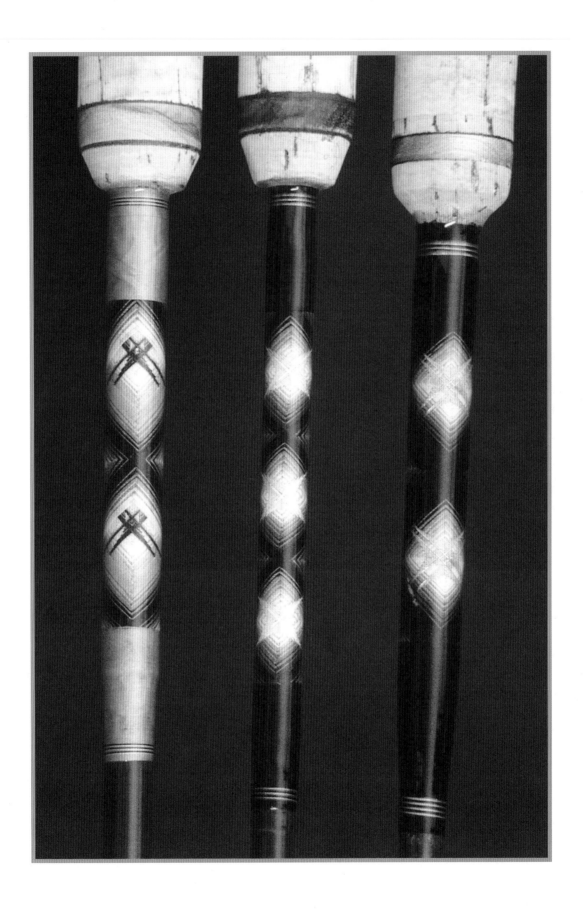

ity, performance and self-confidence in your fishing. Which in the end all actually lead to greater success in your fishing.

This may sound difficult, but actually it is not so complicated. Admittedly a beginner might lack some of the equipment and have little experience, but he can catch up in different ways. There are simple, comprehensible rules and methods to follow that guarantee good results, and everybody can learn, understand and follow them. Obviously certain basic skills are required, but I hope to be able to convey them with this book. And at the same time as you learn to put together a rod, you also learn to check its characteristics.

A large part of the "advantage" of the home crafter is that he has the time. A mass producer has production requirements on him, which means that he has to rationalize, and stages in the building process that are important for performance and quality have to be "cut out" because they take up too much time. A person who is building for himself has all the time in the world, and uses it, because he is the one who is going to have the rod, and the care and attention he puts into it is what makes the difference.

The home crafter also knows exactly what the "customer" wants to have and how the product is to be used. It either concerns a special rod, that can only be obtained by building it yourself, or a rather normal rod adapted to the person and the fishing conditions. A Custom rod, tailor-made for a specific purpose and specific user, will always feel and function better than an "all-round rod".

Moreover, a hand-made rod is the result of a genuine piece of craftsmanship. This means that every joint, every coat of lacquer, and the adjustment of each part are done by hand, and with the precision and carefulness that this enables. A hand-made rod will quite simply last longer.

The positioning of the guides, i.e. the spacing of the guides on the rod blank, is a practical example of what I mean. Mass producers generally use some form of spacing table based on a random sample from the production series. You usually receive this sort of table with building kits, and the guides on all the rods in the series are positioned according to the same table.

Two rod blanks of the same make and model are, however, seldom exactly the same. When the blanks are manufactured there are slight differences in the materials, which for various reasons cannot be avoided without raising the manufacturing price unreasonably. For this reason two otherwise identical rod blanks seldom bend in exactly the same way when exposed to the same load, and where the rod guides should be placed is first and foremost determined by the bending curve of the blank. If the individuality of the blank is correctly used you can utilize its strength to 100 % and then obtain maximum performance.

The only way of finding the correct positioning of the guides for each rod blank is through a series of manual tests – test casting and different loading tests. These are not difficult to do but they can only be done manually, which takes time. No mass producer has the time for manual testing of each rod in their production, so instead of doing this they take random samples and calculate an average spacing, which all the rods are then given regardless of differences in the bending characteristics. It can of course happen that it checks off perfectly, but it is far more common for the positioning of the guides to deviate to a greater or lesser degree from the optimum positioning. In which case the blank is not fully utilized, and in the worst case the guides are so badly positioned that the resulting stress will lead to the rod braking.

On example of how the market for fishing rods governs the characteristics of the rods is in the size of the guides on spinning rods. When the outgoing line reels off the reel's spool in the cast it forms a rather wide spiral, which is pressed outwards by the centrifugal force. This line spiral is pressed together when the line passes through the rod guides and it steals force from the cast, I will return to this when we discuss rod guides later on.

To fully utilize the force in the cast there is actually only one solution – to use a large guide closest to the reel. The problem is, however, that rods with really large guides look clumsy, which makes them difficult to sell. As consumers we are controlled by what attracts the eye, and most of us would prefer to buy a "neat" streamlined rod rather than one that looks heavy and unwieldy.

If you make your living from selling, you adapt to the market. Which is why more or less all spinning rods in the shops have guides that are too small, and will not cast as far as they should be able to do. If anyone should ask why, you can hear things to the effect that new frictionless guide coatings, or the soft and

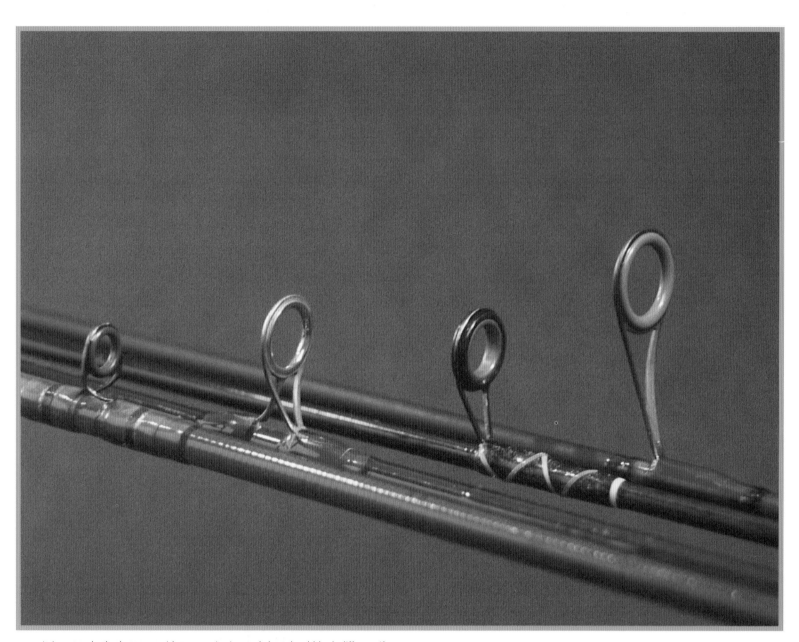

It is not only the bottom guide on a spinning rod that should look different if you are going to achieve maximum performance. To the left a "normal" line guide for a fly rod. The guide to the right of this is higher, which holds the line away from the rod better, and larger, which allows greater freedom of movement for the line and less braking effect. The third guide from the left is a spinning rod guide of "normal height". The high rod guide to the far right is better.

frictionless braided lines, make such guides unnecessary. But as mentioned above the problem is not related to friction, but to the centrifugal force, and as long as the mass of the line cannot be successfully eliminated the centrifugal force remains the same, which also applies to the solution to the problem.

The balance of the rod is another example. A good rod should balance somewhere in the front part of the grip, or just above the grip, i.e. it should be evenly balanced there. An unbalanced rod feels top-heavy and tires out the hand. Anyone who is familiar with the leverage principle will realize that the longer a rod is, the more difficult it is to achieve balance, and that it may be necessary to place weights in the lower part of the grip if it is to be achieved at all.

The increasingly lighter and faster types of graphite the fishing rod market is continuously introducing has put the focus on the weight of the rod – the lighter the better – and a modern one-hand fly rod will soon not have to weigh more than 100 grams. An important and convincing sales argument is that the rod is lighter than other competing rods. The same quick types of graphite are also making increasingly longer one-hand rods more popular, and the longer the rod the more leverage, or balancing weight, that is required.

In actual fact a light, unbalanced rod, is more tiring to use than a heavier, balanced rod. A balanced rod also conveys more feeling for the rhythm of casting, which improves precision and the length of cast, i.e. what can really be important for successful fishing. But as long as the total weight of a rod can be conceived to govern the buyer's choice, the idea of balancing weights in the grip is excluded in commercial manufacturing. In other words lots of rods in the shops are light, but unbalanced.

It is possible to produce other examples of a similar nature, all with the common factor that mass production and the market set requirements on the series producer that prevent him from building his rods with optimum performance, while it is often a simple matter for those who are not driven by market forces to avoid and rectify these problems.

Yet another dimension opens up in the possibilities of special designs. The concept of a Custom rod refers to a rod that is specially adapted, "tailor-made" for one user and one purpose, and something that functions perfectly for that person and precisely what it is intended to be used for.

I have built special rods adapted for transportation in the confined pilot's cockpit in a helicopter, rods for persons with defective vision, with special markings to assist in their assembly, and special grips for personal casting and fishing styles. When I build fly rods I adjust the spine on the blank as a matter of course in relation to the guides, not only to what provides the best performance in general, but to the casting style of the buyer and how he holds his reel and rod in relation to the cast trajectory and his body – so that the positioning of the guides suits precisely his style of casting with the rod. This may sound complicated, but in actual fact it is not, and neither is it difficult to achieve. What it takes is just some reflection, and a total lack of haste. Further on in the book we will discuss these types of adjustments, which everyone, even the beginner, can understand and apply.

Rod blanks - materials and manufacturing

Rule number one for successful rod crafting is never – never build building kits! These are usually made up on the basis of a factory rod as a prototype, which limits the possibilities of achieving a better result than this in many different ways. You need to be able to select the guides, cork and other materials on your own, so that you can achieve the effects you want to have. Building kits do not give you these opportunities.

Building kits also sometimes contain components of inferior quality than those in the "prototype". As we have discussed above the building kit must be sellable, and is put together to meet the generally prevailing opinion that it should be cheap. For successful crafting we must be able to select good materials.

The rod blank is the most important component in a fishing rod, and it is important to choose it with care. For this reason we will now discuss rod blanks and their characteristics in rather considerable detail.

Carbon fiber

Carbon fiber is the only material that does justice to the work you put into building a fishing rod. Because of its lightness and strength it is ideal to make rod blanks from. The stiffness of the fibers, i.e. their resistance to bending, is measured in psi (pounds per square inch). What this unit means in detail is actually unimportant, and we will not go into it – the figures speak so well for themselves anyway. Modern carbon fiber has a bending resistance of 50-60 million psi. Compare this with the best glass fiber types that reach 6 million psi, and the advantages of carbon fiber will be clear enough.

The 8-10 times greater bending resistance of carbon fiber means that a lot less material is needed to achieve the same strength in a carbon fiber blank as in one of another material. A carbon fiber blank has both thinner walls and a smaller diameter than a similar glass fiber blank, and above all it is lighter. A blank of the "first generation" of carbon fiber, now an obsolete material, weighs approximately two-thirds of what an equivalent glass fiber blank weighs. A comparable split cane blade would weigh at least twice as much. Blanks in modern graphite are even lighter.

The weight of the blank, however, usually some ten or so grams, is seldom of any great importance as far as a "normal fishing rod" is concerned. In really long and heavy-duty rods, such as salmon fly rods, it nevertheless does become a different matter. Because of their length these rods have a large leverage effect, and can be tiring to fish with a whole day. If the material in such a rod is light, then this is naturally an advantage.

A very important factor is that the lightness of the material means that the action of a carbon fiber rod can be made faster, and can be varied within wide limits. The inherent mass of the blank becomes less and influences the action less if carbon fiber is used. We will get to the concept of inherent mass later on.

One disadvantage is that the strength of the fibers means that it is not possible to use too much material in the walls of the blank, they would be too stiff. In other words thin walls, which mean that the blanks become less robust, reduce the resistance to wear and increase the risk of breaking the rod, especially on light blanks.

Carbon fiber is produced from some form of fibrous organic polymer (i.e. a substance with threadlike macromolecules). Cellulose (common wood or paper) or rayon can be used. The quality and characteristics of the carbon fibers produced depend among other things on what the molecules in the initial material look like. If the carbon fiber is to be used for rod blanks there are stringent requirements that the fibers should be straight and uniform. The initial material must therefore be as uniform and pure as possible.

When manufacturing carbon fiber for fishing rod blanks a substance called polyacrylonitrile (abbreviated PAN) is used. The transformation to carbon fiber takes place by stretching the PAN fibers and heating them in three stages with increasing temperatures in different gas mixtures. In the first stage the fibers are changed chemically so that they can resist higher temperatures. When the temperature is raised further all the other elements except carbon disappear from the fibers, and finally at over 2,500 degrees the positions of the carbon atoms in the fibers are changed so that what is called the graphite structure is formed. Different types of carbon fibers are achieved by varying the temperature, the gas mixture, and the fiber tension.

Many types of carbon fibers, such as T800 and IM6 etc., are patented products that are available from different chemicals companies, such as DuPont or Union Carbide. They can be bought by anybody and the names themselves have nothing to do with any particular brand of fishing rod, type or action. Both good and bad, fast and slow, rod blanks can be built from the same graphite fibers.

Some newer "graphite designations" are, however, rather more a particular design of fishing rod – a combination of tapering and blank structure, etc. The type of graphite used is for the most part secret, and two different makes of fishing rod could theoretically use exactly the same type of carbon fiber despite the fact that the blanks behave in completely different ways and that there are different designations on the fishing rod labels. The difference lies in completely different aspects, such as how the blank is composed, its tapering, the thickness of the walls, and the different supplementary materials used.

We buyers must in other words not stare ourselves blind at the graphite names. It is wrong to believe that a fishing rod has certain characteristics just because a certain type of carbon fiber is printed on the label. The performance of the fishing rod is determined more by the tapering (the narrowing of the blank) and the thickness of material in the blank, and it is possible to build blanks without the slightest similarity to each other from identically the same type of carbon fiber.

Blanks of carbon fiber

Carbon fiber blanks are manufactured from a carbon fiber weave, where all, or almost all, of the graphite fibers lie in the same direction. A small number, as few as possible, of fibers of another material, such as glass fiber or a softer type of carbon fiber, are woven at right angles to the carbon fibers to hold them together. The weave is impregnated with a thermosetting bonding agent, usually an epoxy resin.

During the manufacturing process the weave is cut to a triangular pattern. The width and narrowing of the pattern determines the amount of material in the blank walls and how this is allocated along the length of the blank. The ready cut weave is rolled up, together with a thin weave of another material – a scrim – on a tapering core or metal mold, a mandrel. The purpose of the scrim is to hold the carbon fibers in position during the curing, so that they do not "wander" and cause annoying irregularities in the distribution of the material round the blank. In modern graphite blanks the scrim also has an effect on the action, e.g. in that it can increase the resistance of the blank to the flattening out that always occurs when the blank is bent, which makes it more rigid. The metal core is turned in a lathe so that the tapering corresponds with the tapering the blank is to have. The tapering and thickness of the walls together determine the action of the blank. The weave is rolled out so that all the graphite fibers end up in the lengthwise direction of the blank. During the curing it is held in position by an outer foil, which is rolled on after the carbon fiber weave.

The curing starts when it is all heated in an oven. Afterwards the core is tapped out of the finished blank and the outer foil is brushed off, and leaves a spiral shaped groove in the surface of the blank. Many manufacturers polish and lacquer the

blank to remove the foil groove purely cosmetically, which hardly makes the blank better. On the contrary, there is a risk of grinding off fibers and weakening the blank, and if anything it is better with a blank that still has the spiral pattern.

The spiral pattern is polished off on most rod blanks, however, after which it is lacquered, sometimes after it has been dyed. Pure carbon fiber has a graphite gray color, so all brown, green, or blanks with another color have been given a surface coating before they are lacquered.

Glossy blanks are always lacquered, which produces a robust and wear-resistant surface. Blanks with a matt surface are for the most part lacquered with a matt lacquer, or polished after lacquering so that the lacquer becomes matt. Sometimes the layer of lacquer on matt blanks is very thin, and on such blanks the fibers that give them their strength lie almost in the surface. This is the actual graphite matt surface of the carbon fibers you can see. For this reason you should be very careful when handling matt blanks and avoid scratching the surface since this can break the fibers and cause weakening.

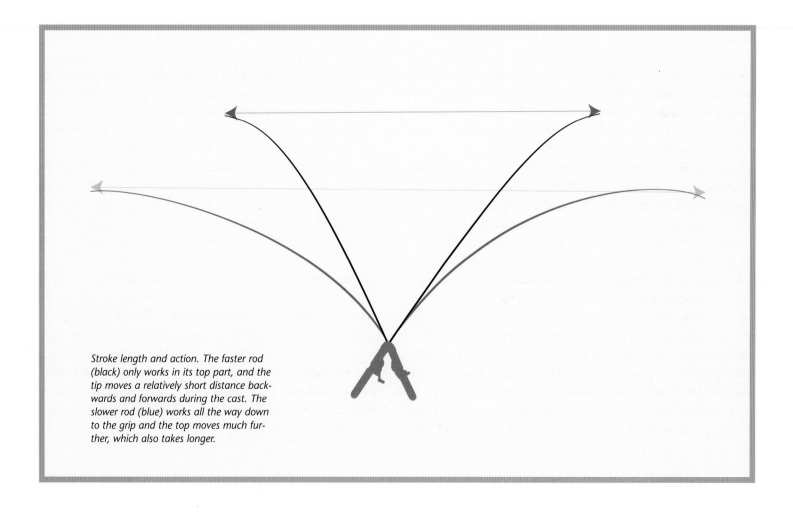

Stroke length and action. The faster rod (black) only works in its top part, and the tip moves a relatively short distance backwards and forwards during the cast. The slower rod (blue) works all the way down to the grip and the top moves much further, which also takes longer.

Action and rod length

When choosing a rod blank you first have to decide how fast you want the rod to work. To discuss this we must first define for each other what we mean by the "speed of the rod".

The concept of the "fastness" or "speed" of a rod refers to how quickly the rod works in a cast, which is related to how much of the blank normally bends when the rod is working. Fast rods are "stiff", work mainly in the top, i.e. a third to a fourth of the blank at the top of the rod is what bends during normal loading. A slow rod on the other hand is "soft", i.e. a large part of the blank is pliant (half, full action). Note that the designations "stiff" and "soft" have nothing whatever to do with the weight of the bait. A rod that casts very heavy weights can be soft/slow, i.e. bend along almost its full length during normal loading. Similarly, an ultra light rod can be stiff/fast, i.e. only a part of the top bends.

To avoid creating confusion I will refrain from using the words "soft" and "stiff" from now on, and instead we will keep to the designations "slow" and "fast". These words are also more correct since they describe how the rod works. For different cast weights we will use the words "light" and "heavy" rod instead.

The designations "fast" and "slow" rod derive from the fact that the cast actually is quicker to perform with a top action rod. A smaller part of the blank is working, the actual cast action is shorter, and the cast therefore takes less time to perform. A slow rod whips further, it takes longer to complete the cast, and it gives a greater margin for variations in the casting rhythm. An inexperienced caster should not choose a rod that is too fast, since its speed sets higher demands on the "timing" and confidence in the casting rhythm. As a rule you can cast further with a fast rod, assuming that you can actually cast with it.

You may think that "fast" rods are stronger than "slow" rods, while in actual fact it is often the reverse. In a full action rod the entire blank absorbs the strain. This is spread out over the complete blank and the risk of the strain on the blank being concentrated to an isolated point is less. In a top action rod a small part of the top of the blank should absorb all the sudden strain and stress. It is therefore easier for it to become concentrated at some particular point, and it is with these sudden spot loads that there is a risk of breaking the rod.

It is possible to bring greater pressure to bear on a fish with a slow rod, and the same applies to short rods in comparison with long rods. To explain this we will have to remember what we learned about leverage in school.

Let us imagine a situation where you are standing and "playing" a fish with the rod butt supported against your stomach. You hold the rod some way up on the grip and point it upwards at an angle of about 45 degrees. The line forms a right angle to the lower part of the rod blank (see illustration), so that the rod and the flexibility of the blank can absorb all the pulls and thrusts. The mechanical situation is such that there are two levers working against each other – one which you pull on, and one which the fish pulls on. Both have the same fulcrum, the point on your stomach against which the butt of the rod is supported.

To be able to raise the rod and pump in the line you have to overcome the torque the fish creates in its direction by pulling on its lever, you quite simply have to create a higher torque in your direction. When your torque and the torque of the fish are equal, the rod is held still, neither drops nor lifts. You can calculate the torque by taking the force either you or the fish is pulling on the respective levers with, and multiplying it by the length of the lever. Only the force acting at right angles to the lever is calculated. For the sake of simplicity we assume here that all the forces are at right angles to the rod.

Your lever (illustration) is the distance along the blank from the butt of the rod to the point where you are holding it with your hand and working to raise the tip of the rod. We can say that it is about half a meter from the butt to your hand if we are talking about a two-hand rod.

The lever of the fish is the distance from the same butt to the line's working point, but since the rod is curved we have to calculate how long this distance is by drawing a line in the direction of the rod, at right angles to the line, and another from the line, so that they meet at an angle of ninety degrees (illustration). The lever of the fish is in other words the distance from the butt to this imagined point.

If the lever of the fish is twice as long as yours it will only feel half the force you are applying on the rod when you bring pressure to bear on it. Or the reverse, if the fish is pulling with a force equivalent to a kilogram you will experience this as twice as much. If the lever of the fish is ten times longer than yours you will feel a force ten times the force the fish is generating, and vice versa. Try this out by hanging a weight from the top of a rod and trying to lift it with the rod. In other words the fish usually feels a lot less force than you think, and even less the longer the rod is.

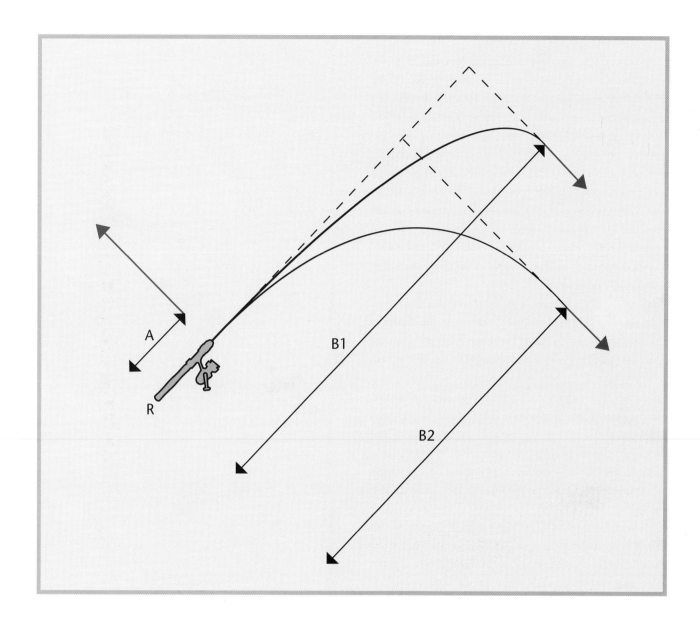

The less the curvature in the rod the further away from you the point of intersection will be, and the longer the lever of the fish (see illustration). The longer the rod you use, the longer the lever of the fish will be. This makes you wonder why it should be better to play salmon on long two-hand rods, and it is the reason why big-game rods are short and have long grips.

Slow rods also compensate for jerks and pitches more smoothly that fast rods, which reduces the risk of the fish pulling free.

It therefore becomes a question of priority. Which characteristics are more important, the length of cast or good playing characteristics?

Power and leverage with rods of different speeds. The point of rotation on the rod (R) is its lower end where the fisherman supports it against his body. The length of lever he has at his disposal (A) is calculated from there up to the point where he holds it when playing the fish. The lever of the fish is the distance from the butt up to the line's working point (B1, B2). The greater the top action a rod has the longer this will be (B1), which gives the fish an advantage.

Parabolic and progressive action

Two concepts of action that often crop up in relation to fly rods are "parabolic" and "progressive" action. You should be aware that these designations do not have anything to do with the casting rhythm of the blank. They rather describe how the rod works when it discharges the force to the bait or line.

A parabolic rod bends and straightens out in approximately the same way as a trampoline. When the jumper lands on the trampoline's apex it bends throughout all its length simultaneously. When the jumper lifts from the trampoline it has straightened out – every centimeter of the trampoline became straight at exactly the same moment, a kind of "explosion" where the blank resumes its linear form at precisely the same moment along its entire length.

If you ask in the shop what progressive action means you often get an answer to the effect that "the more the blank is loaded the further down towards the butt it bends". But all blanks bend deeper down towards the butt the more they are loaded!

A progressive rod works, as opposed to the parabolic, almost like a whip. When you release the cast the blank starts to straighten out at the bottom by the grip, and just like when you crack a whip the force then wanders towards the tip. The straight part of the blank is extended upwards, i.e. the blank "rolls out", until the force is delivered to the bait, more or less like a whiplash.

In other words we are talking about something quite different, namely two different ways of delivering the force from the blank to the bait or line, and which method is best is often discussed in rod crafting circles. Most of the split cane rods have some form of parabolic action, while most modern graphite rods have some form of progressive action.

Parabolic action – progressive action. The top rod has a parabolic action, i.e. the entire rod bends and straightens out at the same time regardless of the pressure it is exposed to, and the curvature is strongest in the lower part of the rod. The lower rod has progressive action, i.e. the greater the pressure on the rod the further down the curvature goes in the rod. The rod straightens out successively from the butt and upwards.

What is it that determines the action?

The action, together with the length, cast weight, and durability of the blank, is one of the characteristics that first and foremost determines the choice of blank. What then is it in the construction of the blank that first and foremost decides which action it has?

- Type of fiber

We have already discussed that the resistance to bending of the fiber material in the blank is important for the action. Above all the stiffness of the fibers decides how much material you need to have in the blank walls to achieve the required strength. In turn the amount of material influences the inherent mass of the blank, which we will discuss further on. The thickness of the wall is also of great importance for the durability of the blank.

- Tapering and wall thickness

In the beginning of the nineties I came across a number of rods that had unexplainably broken without actually having been exposed to any strain. This concerned rods in the upper price class, built of very stiff graphite fiber, which made them very light and gave them a very fast and distinct action. It could have been a simple thing like pulling up the line through the rod guides and then just wanting to draw out a little more line, whereupon the rod broke, in one case at more than one place. It was completely unexplainable, and all these cases came from the same series of rods.

One possible explanation lies in the fact that the very stiff fibers this particular rod series were built from, in combination with the tapering, could have resulted in the walls of the blanks being too thin. In which case the margins for variations in the material thickness could have been too small.

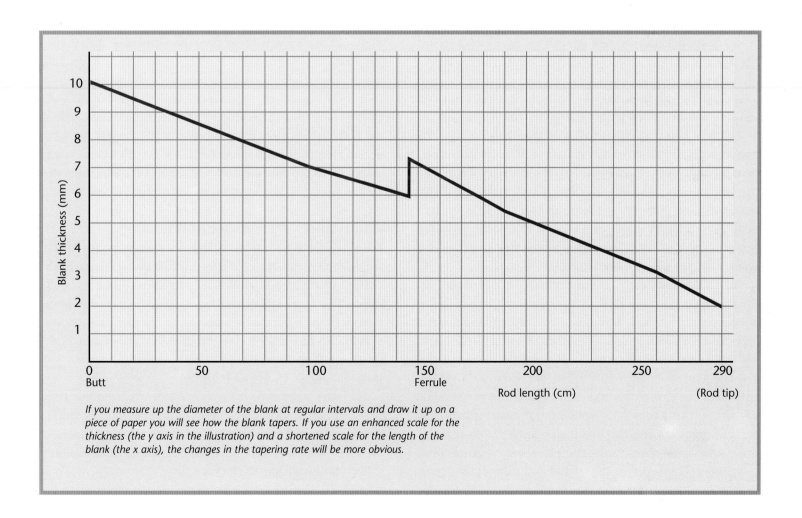

If you measure up the diameter of the blank at regular intervals and draw it up on a piece of paper you will see how the blank tapers. If you use an enhanced scale for the thickness (the y axis in the illustration) and a shortened scale for the length of the blank (the x axis), the changes in the tapering rate will be more obvious.

The wall thickness always varies to a certain degree in all rod blanks, and this is normally experienced in the form of spine effects, which we will discuss later. But in this case a variation in the wall thickness, which admittedly was perhaps a little more robust than usual, but which actually should not have had more impact other than as an unusually robust spine, can have made certain parts of the blank walls so thin that they failed to hold.

The tapering of the blank implies that it narrows from its lower section up to the tip. The tapering is determined by the shape of the metal core, the mandrel, which the graphite weave is wrapped on when the blank is manufactured. The tapering can be straight, by which the blank tapers uniformly from butt to tip, or it can be composed of several different sections with different tapering rates.

It speaks for itself that the smaller the diameter of the blank the easier it is to bend it. If you want to have a blank that bends easily along the greater part of its length you let it quickly taper off in its very lowest part and then continue to taper at a gradually slower rate towards the tip. In this way the blank becomes thin, i.e. already easy to bend in its lower section, after which it continues to have a thin diameter, i.e. easy to bend all the way up to the tip. The blank receives a more or less slow action, i.e. the greater part of it works in the cast.

If instead you manufacture a blank that does not taper to any appreciable extent, or very gradually in its lower section, then the butt section will be stiffer. At some point higher up the tapering rate will increase, which will make the blank quickly thinner there too and in other words make it easier to bend. Such a tapering produces a blank that above all works in the top section, while the butt is more or less stiff. This is a blank with top action, a fast action.

The thickness of the walls on the blank is determined by the tapering in combination with how much graphite weave is wound into the blank. If you cut out a strip of graphite cloth and make a blank with a large diameter from this, the blank will have thin walls. If instead you wind the same strip of graphite weave round a thin mandrel you obtain a thin blank with thick walls. You can achieve the same flexural resistance of a narrow blank with thick walls, that a thinner walled blank with a larger diameter has. The thicker walled, thin blank is more robust and resists scratching more and other mistreatment, but it consumes more material and therefore becomes heavier and has a larger inherent mass.

If you want to measure the tapering of a blank you need a reliable pair of sliding calipers, or even better a micrometer, a ruler, and pen and paper. You quite simply measure the diameter of the blank at regular, rather frequent intervals, for example every five centimeters. Draw it all up by using a ruler on a piece of paper, but exaggerate the width of the blank so that all the diameter figures are increased tenfold, while reducing the length scale at the same time so that the length of the rod on the paper is compressed to perhaps a tenth of the actual length. In this way the tapering becomes exaggerated in the drawing, and it is possible to see with the naked eye any transitions between the sections of the blank that have different tapering rates.

Drawing the tapering is a useful exercise. If you are interested in which factors govern the characteristics of different rods, it is instructive to measure the tapering on rods with different casting characteristics. If you draw up the tapering on a number of rods that you like it is quite possible that you will find clear similarities, which will enable you to more easily assess how you will come to like a certain rod. If you have difficulty in getting hold of a specific blank the measurement of the tapering will make it possible to find a blank with a similar tapering, which means that it has similar bending characteristics.

It is not equally easy to measure the thickness of the walls on the blank since this requires precision measurements inside the blank. The weight of the blank can be a certain help, but actually the only functioning method is saw the blank up into sections and measure the thickness of the wall, something that we can perhaps postpone until the continuation course.

- Resistance of the blank to flattening

When a tube is bent there is always a certain degree of flattening. The material in the tube walls is stretched out in the outside of the bend, while it is pressed together along the inside. This cannot take place to any degree whatsoever, in the outside of the bend the tube provides resistance to the expansion and in the inside to the compression. This results in the tube becoming flattened out to a greater or less extent – soft metal tubes will also bend in the end.

The same applies to the graphite tubes constituting a rod blank. The cross section of a bent blank is more or less oval in shape, the extent to which mainly depends on the thickness of the tube walls since thick walls resist flattening more than thin walls. If the blank does not have a large tendency to become oval then it will be stiffer and resist flexural forces, while if it easily

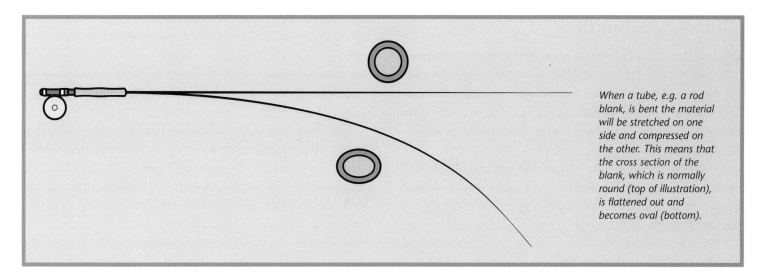

When a tube, e.g. a rod blank, is bent the material will be stretched on one side and compressed on the other. This means that the cross section of the blank, which is normally round (top of illustration), is flattened out and becomes oval (bottom).

becomes oval it will be softer. The thickness of the blank walls influence its tendency to become oval, and in this way its action.

There are ways of increasing the resistance of a soft blank to flattening. Reinforcing bushings of light material can be glued in the blank for example to hold its cross section round, or it can be reinforced externally with wraps or the like. One should, however, be careful with such experiments. The blank will certainly become stiffer where the reinforcements are located, but strain can occur at other places on the blank where there are no reinforcements and in unfortunate cases, if the strength of the material is not sufficient, this can result in the blank breaking.

- Inherent mass

The inherent mass is the mass of the material in the actual blank. You might then wonder what mass is, and if it is the same as what the blank weighs? You will notice the weight of the blank when you carry or hold the rod, while you will notice the mass when you move it. When performing a casting movement the rod bends because the mass, which accelerates during the casting movement, has inertia, i.e. wants to counteract the acceleration and remain in the initial position. The mass that accelerates is the total of the mass of the bait/line and the mass of the rod, i.e. the mass of the blank, guides, wraps, and lacquer etc. When the rod straightens out to send away the bait/line the stiffness of the blank, its tendency to straighten out, must counteract the inertia of both its inherent mass and the mass of what it is sending away.

The less the inherent mass of the rod, the more capacity the

fibers it is built from will have to send away the bait, and the quicker it will go. Material used to increase the strength of the rod also increases its inherent mass, which makes the rod heavier and more clumsy, and produces the opposite effect so that the action is braked. The inherent mass in the blank material sets a limit for the speed of the action that can be achieved.

Test curve

The concept of a test curve is also used in this connection, mainly for rods that are not primarily used to cast with, such as fishing rods, sea fishing rods and trolling rods. The test curve was described on an Internet page I saw as "a funny way of describing the action, that an Englishman has come up with", but the concept does not in fact refer to the action of the rod at all.

The test curve concept is measured in units of weight, such as lbs, kg or the like. To find a rod's test curve you fix its butt end in a horizontal position and then weigh down the tip of the rod until it points straight down, i.e. at a right angle to the rod butt. The mass that the blank must be loaded with to do this is called the blank's test weight or test curve.

This concept describes the strength of the blank, but not its action. It is no problem to find both fast and slow blanks that require the same load to bend the tip at a right angle to the butt. The difference is only that the slow blank bends along its entire length, while the bending in the fast top action blank only takes place in a short section of its top. But they both bend so that the top points at right angles to the butt. The test curve is an indication of how the blank can handle heavy bait weights and loads.

Choosing a blank

Since a bare blank differs quite considerably from the finished rod the choice of blank should be made with due care. Formulate a number of basic requirements you want to set for your prospective rod. Specify the required length, cast weight and action, i.e. the casting and playing characteristics, as carefully as possible.

The choice of rod length is largely determined by practical issues. Long rods cast longer than short ones – you get higher a speed up on the bait – but this does not mean that rods can be too long because the longer the lever, the greater the inertia. There is a limit at which an increase in the length of rod actually leads to lower rod tip speed and consequently a shorter cast. This depends of course on how strong you are, but for a one-hand rod the limit usually lies somewhere around 9-10 feet.

It is easier to control the fish with a long rod, but long rods also get in the way sometimes, and it is more difficult to go in and fish in dense vegetation with a long rod. If you are going to land or gaff a fish it is more difficult to get it within reach if the rod is very long, especially when fishing from a boat. Long rods are also more difficult to transport. And finally, we have already considered the effect the rod length has on how hard you can manage to press the fish when playing it. Think through all this and decide which considerations are most important for your rod.

Judging the action

This is how a lot of people judge a rod before a prospective purchase. They pick out a rod from the rack in the shop, and standing among the shelves in what is often a rather confined space they aim down the length of the blank, flick the rod a few times and weigh it in their hand. If there is enough space they might make a few quick casts. With the information gathered from this they then decide whether to buy the rod or not.

None of the above maneuvers give any whatsoever reliable information on the characteristics of the blank.

If you are going to buy a ready-made rod there are three main things to think about. First whether the action is right, i.e. if the speed of the blank suits your skill as a caster, and the requirements for the casting and playing characteristics you set for the rod. Secondly, if the rod guides are placed on the correct side of the blank in relation to its spine, and thirdly, that the relative spacing of the guides is sufficient to distribute the strain uniformly over the entire rod. The two latter prerequisites are what we can guarantee by building the rod correctly. Point number one is the most important when buying a rod blank.

The best way of judging the characteristics of the blank is of course by test casting with the rod. Good fishing tackle shops offer their customers the opportunity to do this, but this is not always the case. If you are buying a rod blank then the rod has to be assembled before you can cast with it, unless of course there is an identical one ready to use. How then can the action of a blank be assessed when you cannot actually cast with the rod? You have to look at the blank's bending curve, and there are two main methods of doing this. We call them the static and the dynamic methods.

The static method (see illustration - page 17) is done by fixing the butt end of the blank in some way so that the rod points upwards at an angle of about 45 degrees. You then weigh down the tip until the rod is "normally loaded" and study how the blank bends. You can for example let a friend hold the blank, while someone else pulls down the tip, while you study the curvature from the side. Note that the blank's ferrules must be reinforced so that they do not crack! Wrap them with thread and apply color preservative. In acute cases you can wrap a few turns of tape tightly round the female ferrule!

A full-action blank has an angle of curvature that stretches along its entire length. The curve becomes more flattened towards the grip, but no part of the curve is completely flat when the blank is loaded. If the lower part of the blank is straight and the bend begins approximately half way towards the tip, it has a half-action – slightly faster. A fast blank only works in the top section – the bending starts over the "mid line".

When dynamically judging a blank you hold it pointing horizontally straight in front of you with both hands, and with the butt end firmly supported against your stomach. Now set the rod tip swinging from the right to the left and try to find a "rhythm" where the blank swings "by itself". The blank will now only be loaded by its inherent mass while it swings backwards and forwards. Since the swinging is continuously repeated you can now study to blank's angle of curvature from "above" (illustration). At the same time you can feel

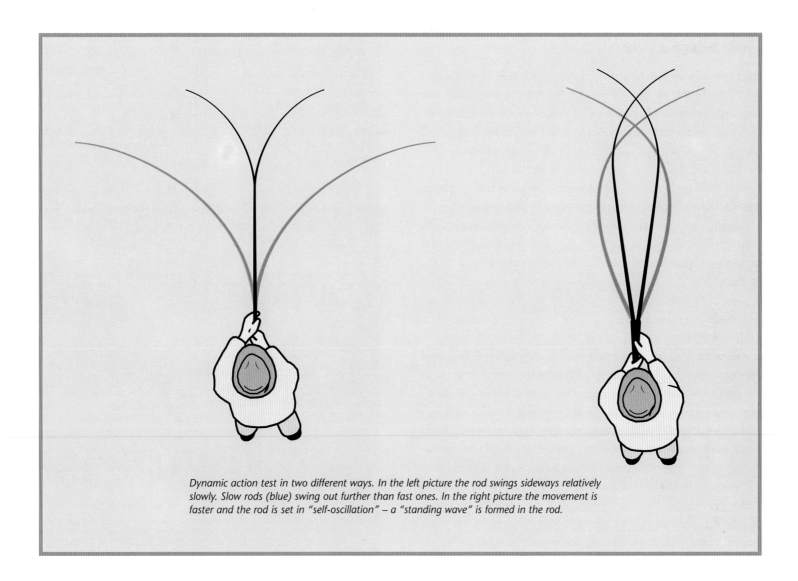

Dynamic action test in two different ways. In the left picture the rod swings sideways relatively slowly. Slow rods (blue) swing out further than fast ones. In the right picture the movement is faster and the rod is set in "self-oscillation" – a "standing wave" is formed in the rod.

how quickly the rod is working – a slow blank has a slower "rhythm" in its swinging than a top-action blank.

You can also try swinging the blank faster and try to find a rhythm where the blank swings out in a "bulge" close to you and almost stands still (node) a little closer to the tip (illustration). The bulge becomes deeper and the node comes closer the slower the blank is, while the actual swinging also goes more slowly.

Take the time to try out these methods of assessment in front of the rod rack in your fishing tackle shop. Test both fast and slow and rods, i.e. both on top-action rods and those with full-action. The more experience you acquire the easier it is to judge a new blank later. Bear in mind also that a bare blank is always faster than a finished rod! Guides, wraps and lacquer increase the inherent mass, which makes the rod slower.

Reel seats

A reel seat normally consists of a sleeve or a tube, e.g. of metal – a body, which all the other reel seat parts are placed on. It is normally threaded in one end, and in the other end has a house cap, i.e. a fixed sleeve that holds one end of the reel foot. A second, flexible sleeve, cap or locking sleeve, is screwed to the reel foot by means of one or two lock nuts. At the bottom end of a fly rod reel seat there is a butt, a knob of cork, wood or rubber, that provides protection from contact with the ground.

The reel seat can also be designed so that two loose rings, sliding rings, slide on a body of, for example, cork. These are pressed together over the reel foot from each side and lock it to the cork.

Threads

The thread on a reel seat can be manufactured in several different ways. If it is metal you thread it with a die in the same way you would a bolt, or turn the thread in a lathe, or press in the thread in the reel seat body. For press threading to function the reel seat must be made of relatively thin and soft plate. Turning and cut threading is also used on wooden reel seats. If the reel seat is made of some form of rubber material, e.g. graphite plastic, then the thread is of course molded at the same time as the reel seat body.

Threads made with dies are durable and maintain a higher finish, but are almost only to be found on hand-made reel seats. In mass production the threads are usually turned/ milled or pressed. What mainly determines the durability and function of the reel seat is its material thickness and the thread profile.

Turned/milled threads often have a trapezoid profile, i.e. the cross-section of each "thread ridge" is square. Trapezoid threads are very durable since they do not round-off and become thinner upwards towards the ridge of the thread. Reel seats with turned threads are most often made in relatively strong materials and have a high finish. This method is expensive and is used for more exclusive reel seats.

Pressed threads normally have a rounded shape, the cross-section resembles a water wave (sine curve). You can easily see that the thread is pressed into the metal since the thread pattern can also be seen on the inside of the tube. Press threading is an inexpensive and quick manufacturing method that is common on simple reel seats. Since the material must be thin for it to be shaped, such reel seats can often become distorted

when exposed to stress. This type of reel seat should be avoided except on very light rods.

On threads with a rounded shape the nut can "glide up" towards the thread ridge when tightening, and you can get threads that "play over" or lock.

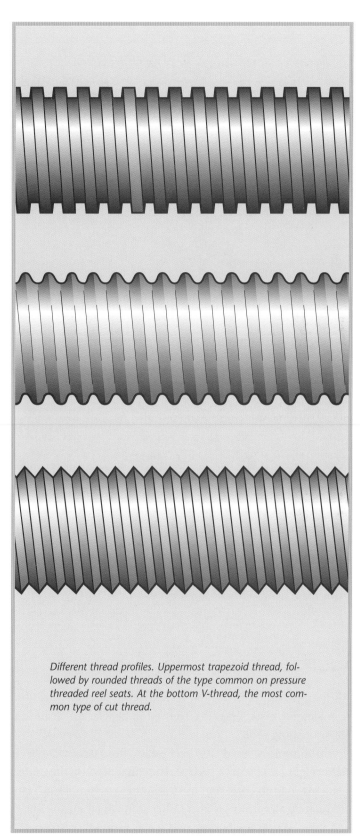

Different thread profiles. Uppermost trapezoid thread, followed by rounded threads of the type common on pressure threaded reel seats. At the bottom V-thread, the most common type of cut thread.

Modern fly rod reel seat. From the left a stainless steel reel seat with full-metal body for saltwater fishing, anodized aluminum reel seat with wooden insert, and two full-metal reel seats, the left with recess for a fighting butt and double lock rings for heavier fishing. Below these, lighter reel seats for mounting on combinations of cork and wood.

Different types of reel seats. At the top from the left a nickel silver reel seat, reel seat of graphite plastic and a pair of different types of metal reel seats, divided up to be provided with inserts of wood or cork. Under the nickel silver reel seat, factory-made wooden inserts. At the bottom, hand-made inserts – from left to right first of wooden rings and then solid. In the middle, sections that are to be glued and turned to reel seat inserts.

Metals in reel seats

Aluminum, nickel silver, and recently even titanium, are used to make reel seats. Brass is also used in heavier reel seats, e.g. for sea fishing rods.

Aluminum is used for reel seats on light rods, it is lightweight and forms a surface oxide that protects the underlying metal from corrosion in "freshwater environments". Unfortunately aluminum is also rather soft, which means that is can be relatively easily distorted when exposed to stress. For

this reason you should choose aluminum reel seats made in relatively thick material.

Aluminum is surface treated in several different ways, and lacquering and anodizing are common methods when manufacturing reel seats. Lacquered reel seats are easily scratched, and it can happen that the lacquer can shed. Anodizing is a more expensive and better method of surface treatment, which means that the coloring pigment is bonded to the aluminum's surface oxide by means of an electrochemical process. The color goes deep down into the hard oxide layer, which also becomes extra strong, and which also means that both the color and corrosion resistance become very durable.

Nickel silver is used for reel seats on more "luxurious fly rods". This is an alloy of nickel and iron that chemically resembles stainless steel, but which has a silver-like gloss and is easy to work. On the other hand as opposed to stainless stain, nickel steel oxidizes rather easily and it happens that the lock nuts

A bare graphite reel seat is not particularly attractive on its own, but can be built up with wood or cork so that it suits even more exclusive rods.

become coated with verdigris and "jam" if the reel seat is exposed to moisture for a prolonged period. You always have to look after a rod with a nickel silver reel seat very carefully and protect it from moisture, which can be a problem with fishing tackle.

Titanium is an ideal material for reel seats, it has the lightness of aluminum but is not equally soft and as easily deformed. Titanium reel seats are surface treated through anodizing in exactly the same way as aluminum, and this gives them a wear-resistant and robust surface with an attractive finish.

Brass is a ductile and durable metal alloy with a heavy and solid feeling. It does, however, oxidize rather easily. Even if this does not usually affect its function, the metal darkens and becomes ugly. For this reason it is common to chrome brass reel seats, and sometimes the chrome has a tendency to shed.

Graphite plastic

The best reel seats available on the market in terms of their function are actually the quite inexpensive types of graphite plastic reel seats used on many rods in the economy class. "Fuji reel seats" – the Japanese Fuji made the original – are available in a large number of makes, and graphite plastic reel seat is a more correct name. The plastic is reinforced with graphite fibers, and the same type of material is also used for keepers and spools on fishing reels.

Graphite plastic is strong and wear-resistant, withstands cold and heat within normal limits, and the plastic is an insulator that makes it easier to keep warm in the winter than metal, since it does not conduct heat and therefore does not become equally cold to hold. Plastic does not of course oxidize, and in spite of their lightness these types of reel seats are often strong enough to also be used on heavier rods. There again the disadvantage is their look – with a gray and dull color – but an insert of wood or cork can produce a really attractive reel seat.

Watch out for poor imitations – there are a large number of makes and models of the graphite plastic reel seats, some completely without graphite in the plastic, and in other words a significant variation in the quality. There are those that is terms of function are equivalent with the Fuji original, while others function considerably worse even if they exactly resemble a Fuji reel seat. Fuji's series FPS and FPSDM have the insides of the sleeves coated with plastic, which is beneficial for the reel and holds it more securely.

Skeleton reel seat with insert of cork and wood. The insert, to the right, is glued on the blank between the house cap, at the top in the illustration on the reel foot, and the thread body, at the bottom. It forms one unit and fits well in the hand.

Wood

On reel seats with threads and the body made of wood you obviously avoid all risk of corrosion, but instead you have a material that in untreated condition absorbs water. A wooden reel seat that absorbs water will at the best only swell up enough for the nut to jam, and it will then have to dry out before the reel can be removed. At the worst the wood may crack when it dries, or also the surface treatment may not let the moisture out again, and the reel seat will rot. In other words it is important find out exactly how the reel seat has been surface treated. Most of the ready-made wooden reel seats are deep-impregnated with epoxy resin. In addition to providing protection from moisture, the epoxy resin binds together the wood fibers so that the material becomes harder, which reduces the risk of pulling apart the threads.

One way of making a standard reel seat more personal is to provide it with an insert of cork or wood. A graphite reel seat can in this way be made to fit a more exclusive rod. It becomes a reel seat that combines reliable function with an attractive appearance, something that is otherwise not too easy to find. Wood inserts complete with the accompanying reel seats can of course be bought, but you obtain a more personal reel seat and one that better fits the rod and reel if you make it yourself. Even here there is the above mentioned problem with wood and moisture, but two-component lacquers correctly used can produce a very strong and resistant surface. I use floor lacquers of both the one and two-component types to surface treat wooden and horn parts, and so far this has functioned without any problems at all even on rods that are handled carelessly.

I will go into how cork and wood is turned further on. If you are thinking of having an insert in the reel seat you cut off the smooth, unthreaded part of its body so that you obtain two parts, the house cap on a piece of the body that is just enough to go under it, and a thread, just long enough for the reel to be put and taken off. This type of reel seat is called a skeleton reel seat.

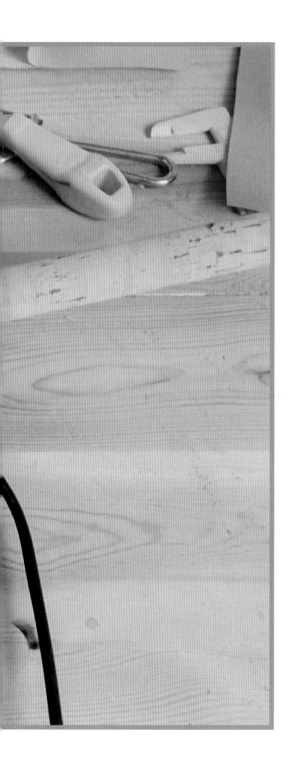

Sizes and functions

The reel seat should only be large enough to hold the reel. Unnecessarily large reel seats take up far too much space on the grip and end up having a "gripping function", i.e. you end up holding the reel seat instead of the grip, which for the most part is both uncomfortable and provides an inferior grip. An unnecessarily large reel seat can give rise to lateral play in the reel.

You should therefore choose a reel seat that is only large enough to allow the reel foot to go into the sleeves, and when you are building the rod you can cut it down to just the right length to allow the reel to be taken off. By this means you have minimized the reel seat surfaces in the grip.

On the other hand you ought to avoid having the diameter of the reel seat too small. The underside of the reel foot is recessed in such a way that it will follow the curvature of the reel seat body. If the curvature of these two surfaces do not more or less correspond this can easily lead to a reel seat made of thin material becoming distorted when you tighten, and it can also happen that the sleeves lock over the reel foot. On reels with feet of graphite plastic there is also a risk that parts on the end of the reel foot can be knocked loose as a result of the force applied to the different curvatures when the reel seat is tightened.

The size of the reel seat is given as the inner diameter of the reel seat. On most fly rods it is sufficient with a 16 mm reel seat, while on two-hand rods the slightly larger 18 mm is often just right. The diameter of the blank where the reel seat is to sit determines of course the minimum possible inner diameter. On light casting and spinning rods 16 mm is also very good, with 18 mm for slightly heavier rods and two-hand rods. The larger reel seats of up to 20 mm in diameter and above are as a rule only needed on really heavy-duty rods, such as sea fishing rods and the like.

It is always good to choose a reel seat with double lock nuts. The second nut secures the first so that the locking sleeve will not come loose when the rod is used.

The length of the reel seat should be just right. If as in the illustration it is longer than what is needed to provide space for the reel, it can be shortened.

Grips

On casting and spinning rods the grip consists of two parts, with the reel seat somewhere in the middle. The top part – the fore grip – is usually shorter than the bottom part – the butt grip. On two-hand fly rods, which also have grips consisting of two parts, the butt grip is shortest. One-hand fly rods only have one grip part, and possibly a fighting butt under the reel seat.

In the top end of the rod grip there is sometimes a winding check, or check ring, that seals and connects to the rod blank. At the bottom of the grip there is a butt. On a one-hand fly rod the lower end connects to the reel seat.

Generally speaking all one-hand fly rods, even in the lightest line classes, benefit from having the so-called fighting butt at the bottom, a short grip part of 3-6 cm located below the reel seat. This makes it possible to support the rod against the wrist, the stomach or somewhere else when you are playing fish and your arm begins to tire. The butt also ensures that the reel comes up a bit from the ground when you set the rod down, which protects it from dirt and moisture and also simplifies balancing the grip if you need to glue in balancing weights.

The grip can also be fitted with decorative rings of, for example, special hardwood or trim rings, and these can also be used as connections or transitions between different grip parts, or between the grip and reel seat. Trim rings can be made from different types of wood, horn, leather, and hard or soft plastic materials, to name a few examples.

A butt finishes off the grip at the bottom, a check ring to the top. You can buy ready-made ones, but you can just as well make them from wood or cork. In the illustration, check rings, butts and other wooden parts in masur birch.

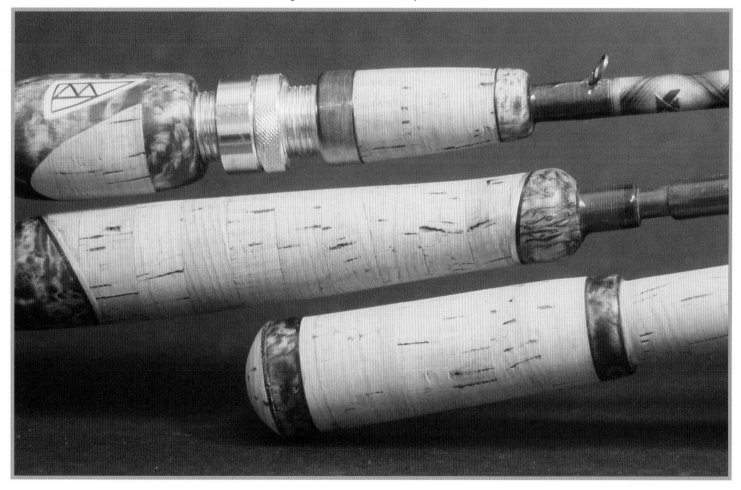

Grip cork

Cork is the outer bark of cork oak (Quercus suber), which is harvested about every tenth year, and Portugal is the leading producer on the world market. The quality depends on the thickness of the bark when it is harvested. The wine industry is a large consumer of cork and a lot of the quality cork ends up there, which means that really good cork is unfortunately difficult to get hold of. Because of the extensive demand the bark on the cork oaks is often harvested before it has become thick enough to make good grip cork.

Poor cork is full of holes, cracks and hard sections. Apart from its drab appearance this type of cork has inferior durability and the irregularities make it more difficult to shape an attractive grip. It is not comfortable to hold and the cork does not last as long. Good grip cork should be as pure, uniform and tight as possible. The highest quality grade is usually designated FLOR, followed by the grades AAA and AA, which is probably the limit for what can be used for building rods. The quality then drops from A and down the alphabet.

Any holes and blemishes can be seen by inspecting both the flat sides of the cork ring. The rounded surfaces say basically nothing because all the pores go from flat side to flat side. It is worth inspecting each cork ring separately and very carefully when buying cork. Most of the holes and irregularities are to be found on the side of the cork that has lain outermost in the bark, and a cork ring that looks good on one side can be full of holes on the other. For the same reason you should avoid buying cork parts that are glued together from several pieces, such as pre-glued grip sections or ready-made grips. A faultless surface often conceals holes and irregularities.

Other grip materials

The shortage of good cork has encouraged replacement materials, and nowadays there are several different grip materials of the cellular plastic type in the grip. These are usually ductile and easy to polish and they are available in many different colors so that there are plenty of opportunities to achieve color-matching designs of various types. However, it is doubtful if you can get the same "feeling" in a cellular plastic grip as in a cork grip. Above all watch out for over soft materials – a grip that feels too soft when you are holding it becomes uncomfortable and tiring to hold.

Cork rings of different qualities. At the far left FLOR cork, then so-called "first" or AAA cork, and at the far right A cork. The quality varies between different manufacturers. FLOR cork is now almost impossible to get hold of.

parts of the grip, or even all of it, are made in a slightly heavier material than cork, especially those parts that lie below the "balancing point", this will create a natural balance and reduce the need for weights.

All types of wood can be used for reel seats and grip effects, it is only a question of getting hold of attractive wood. Many sports shops sell wood for carving, and teak, mahogany and sometimes walnut can be found at your usual lumber dealer. You should, however, make sure that it is cultivated wood and does not come from some rainforest or other, bearing in mind the plundering of the rainforests in progress today.

Cutlers sell grip sections in curly-grained birch and a large number of other species of wood. Why not an inset of horn, birch bark and leather as in Nordic knife handles.

Left: Materials for making cellular plastic grips are available in every conceivable color. Different parts are glued together with contact adhesive, and there are an infinite number of opportunities to create different patterns and color combinations.

Below: Fly rod grip of materials taken from Nordic knife crafting. Wooden parts in stained masur birch, engraved inserts, and reel seat of reindeer horn. Inserts of leather and tin.

For those people who are creative and want to test different alternatives to cork as a grip material, carving is a closely associated handicraft that ought to be able to provide a lot of ideas. Different species of wood have long been used for decorative rings and inserts in fishing rod grips, so why not develop this and experiment with larger sections or even complete grips built from wood, birch bark, leather or other similar materials. Birch bark, for example, has a lot in common with cork in that it provides good friction when you hold it, is warm to hold, and also relatively light, which is an advantage in a rod grip.

On the other hand a grip with a little weight does not need to a disadvantage. We have already touched upon the concept of balance and confirmed that quite a lot of rods need balancing weights in the bottom of the grip to avoid becoming top-heavy. A light, but top-heavy rod is in general more tiring to cast with than a heavy, well-balanced one. If

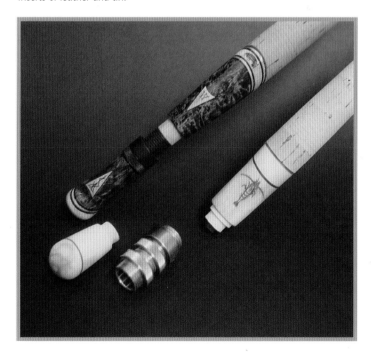

Rod guides influence the action

After the rod blank the rod guides are the absolutely most important components on a rod. Good rod guides have low friction to the line and they are high, large, light and flexible. They must of course be of the type and number that function on the rod you build, and above all they must be placed in such a way that the characteristics of the blank can be utilized optimally. Positioning the guides correctly on the rod is, so to speak, the very essence of successful rod crafting, and we will go into this subject more thoroughly a little further ahead.

The rod guides change the action of the blank through their very existence, and to be able to choose the guides for your rod you need to know how a set of rod guides influences its characteristics. This basically takes place in two different ways, and depending on the type of guides, their size and number, one or the other will predominate and lead to variable consequences. For each new rod guide project it is important to determine which effect is going to dominate, i.e. in which direction the action will be changed.

In most cases it is naturally best if the action of the blank is affected as little as possible. Sometimes, however, you will want to achieve changes in one or the other direction, and an experienced rod crafter can utilize the guide spacing and choice of guides to make the rod faster or slower.

The inherent mass increases

The mass of the guides is added on to the mass of the blank and in other words increases the total inherent mass. When casting, the rod must be able to handle both the weight of the bait and its own inherent mass – this is a subject we have discussed before. A large inherent mass makes the rod smoother and slower, while at the same time a larger part of the capacity of the blank is needed to move the rod's inherent mass in the cast, so that there is less left over to cast away the bait or the line. This implies a reduction of the upper limit for the bait weight the line can handle when casting.

In other words you get a slower rod with a slightly lower casting capacity, and if you want to avoid this you will therefore have to use light rod guides. If on some occasion you have reason to "slow down" a rod that is too fast, you can try using a heavy set of rod guides and also place them higher up on the rod – this increases the inherent weight to maximum. But you should bear in mind that the casing capacity of the rod can be reduced. More about positioning of the guides further ahead.

Lightness and flexibility

The feet and keepers on the rod guides are less flexible than the rod blank. The parts of the blank that are wrapped tight to a guide foot therefore become more rigid sections in the rod. Moreover, each wrap implies an additional support that helps the tubular blank to resist the tendency to "flatten out" or become oval when it is bent, something which also makes the blank stiffer. This effect is in most cases less pronounced than the above mentioned effect of the mass of the guides on the inherent mass of the rod, but it exists.

The rod therefore becomes "faster" and its angle of curvature is interfered with. The former can be utilized constructively, while an angle of curvature that is interfered with can result in spot loads and the risk of the rod breaking, and should therefore be avoided if possible. If you want to try and increase the speed of the blank you can try putting very light guides on the rod and wrapping them tight with long wraps, which are very lightly lacquered to avoid the mass of the lacquer increasing the inherent mass. Good rod guides are therefore flexible and follow the movement of the blank.

The mass of the guides

Ceramic guides are among the heaviest there are, and above all it is the steel keepers that the ceramic guides sit in that make them heavy. Single-footed guides have less metal in the keeper than double-footed guides and are of course lighter. They function well for most rods except for the very heaviest. If the ceramic guide should be mounted in a middle ring of rubber, this would clearly increase the mass. A ceramic guide glued directly in the keeper is sensitive to knocks, but both the guide and keeper can made more slender.

Ceramic rod guides with titanium keepers are manufactured by FUJI. Titanium has a density of 4.5 g/cm3 compared with 7.8 for steel, and they are almost half as heavy. The lightness and hardness of the material make it perfect for manufacturing rod guides. A ceramic rod guide with a titanium keeper is almost equally light as a snake guide in the same size.

Friction and size

If the rod does not cast as far as it should this is in most cases because the line is braked in one way or the other when it passes through the guides. Worn and uneven guides both brake and wear the line. Good guides should therefore be made of the most frictionless (smooth and polishable) and wear-resistant material possible.

Rod guides should also often be larger than you would think, to reduce the braking of the line when you are casting. Both casting and spinning rods deliver the line with some form of side movement. On their way through the guides the line bulges are successively dampened or "constrained" until the line finally becomes straight when it leaves the tip of the rod. Large line bulges pressed through small guides are the reason for the most important, and the most easily influenced, line braking effect from the rod guides.

Note that this problem has very little to do with friction! Friction naturally also has an effect on the line speed, but in this case the effect is much less than you might be led to believe. What steals force when the line spiral from an open-face reel is pressed together in order to go through a narrow rod guide is the centrifugal force that must be developed to compress the spiral.

I would like to clarify this and use the line that goes off an open-face reel when casting as the basis for my reasoning. You could say that the line spiral turns, while actually it resembles a three-dimensional sine wave that moves forwards along the rod. The turning motion of the line spiral presses it out from the center. It can be compared (actually it is not a real force) with a force that pulls the spiral apart – centrifugal force (centri + fugere = to flee). We are all familiar with this and experience it for example when driving through a curve in the car. The greater the mass of the line (= thick line) and the higher the line speed, the more powerful the centrifugal force.

To counteract the centrifugal force and press the line spiral together until it becomes narrow enough to go through the rod guide requires an opposing force. This is a real force, a centripetal force, and it pulls the line spiral together towards its center. It must be greater than the centrifugal force in order to overcome it. The centripetal force is the force that, for example, the friction of the tires develop to the road and which holds the car in the curve.

In the case of an open-face reel the force is developed by the rod guides in contact with the line. The guides constrict the line so that it can be pressed through. The line is forced

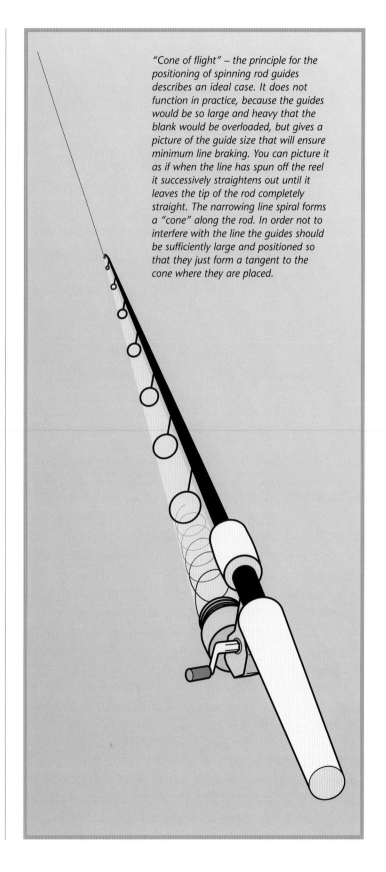

"Cone of flight" – the principle for the positioning of spinning rod guides describes an ideal case. It does not function in practice, because the guides would be so large and heavy that the blank would be overloaded, but gives a picture of the guide size that will ensure minimum line braking. You can picture it as if when the line has spun off the reel it successively straightens out until it leaves the tip of the rod completely straight. The narrowing line spiral forms a "cone" along the rod. In order not to interfere with the line the guides should be sufficiently large and positioned so that they just form a tangent to the cone where they are placed.

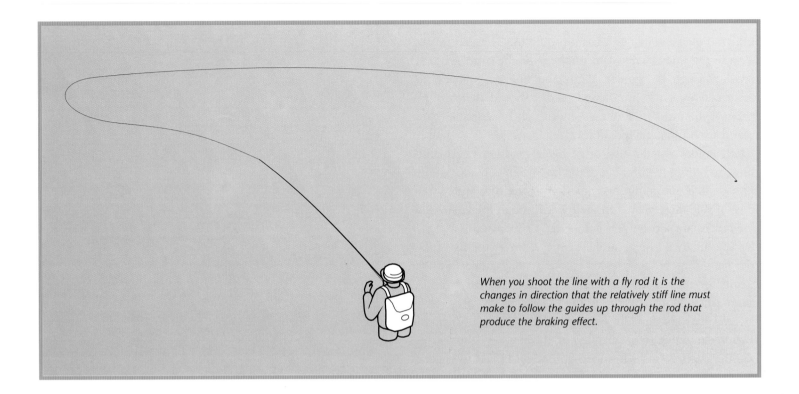

When you shoot the line with a fly rod it is the changes in direction that the relatively stiff line must make to follow the guides up through the rod that produce the braking effect.

into a narrow path – against the centrifugal force. When it does this it looses kinetic energy – it is braked – and this is because the centripetal force steals energy from the cast, i.e. not in the first instance from friction between guide and line. If the guides have a high friction to the line the effect will of course be greater, but it cannot be eliminated with frictionless guide material, only by large guides that allow the line spiral to be stretched out and narrow off by itself, instead of a small first guide forcefully pressing the spiral together at once. The line from a casting rod is influenced in approximately the same way, with the difference that the sine wave here is two-dimensional – from side to side – and the effect is less.

Fly rods function a little differently. The line is shot from the hand, a line basket or the surface of the water. In this case it is in the points in the line trajectory where the direction of the line is changed that the greatest braking effect takes place, and therefore friction is a more important factor. The change of direction is mainly at the line guide and is minimized with the correct guide positioning. Fly rods intended for winter fishing should have larger guides than normal to avoid icing up.

Height of the guides

On fly rods the friction to the blank is of great importance for the casting length, in many cases more than the friction to the guides. Wet lines that stick and drag along the blank can lead to very powerful line braking, and above all in the back cast the line is pressed against the blank. Line braking in this situation prevents the line from sliding up through the guides when we release in the double stroke. This reduces our possibilities of performing effective double pulls and shooting out the line well. The height of the fly rod guides is therefore, contrary to general opinion, very important.

The fact that the line is strongly braked if it drags along blank applies to all types of rods, and all rod guides must be high enough to hold the line away from the blank. This applies both when casting and when playing fish – if the line rubs against the blank under pressure it can cause the line to break

In general most of the mass produced rods have too small, and often too low guides. If the rod can handle it, it is always a good idea to go up at least one number in the size of guides compared to an equivalent rod in the shop.

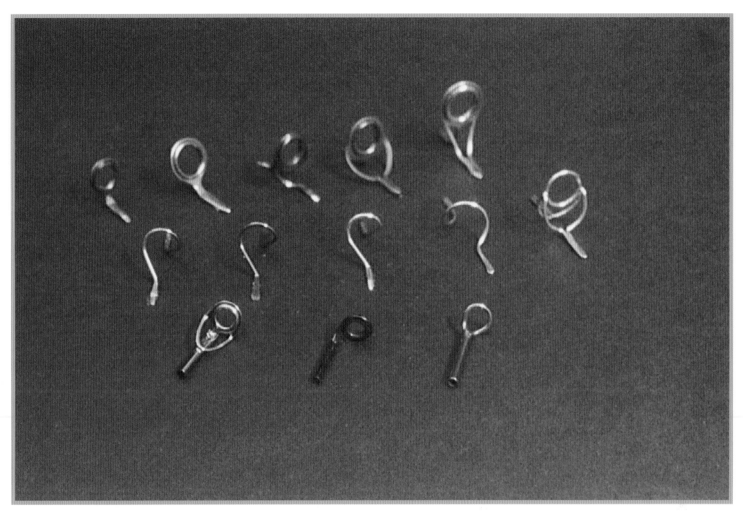

Guides for fly rods. In the back row ceramic guides, from the left single leg guide with standard ceramic and steel keeper, single leg guide with SIC ceramic and titanium keeper, and three guides suitable as line guides. In the middle, snake and metal guides: to the left an American model with titanium nitride, one with titanium carbide and a chromed guide. The fourth from the left is an English model (turned to the left instead of the right). To the far right a bridge guide. In the foreground from the left a SIC titanium eye with support leg, a standard eye without support leg and a drop-eye with titanium nitride.

Guides – types, materials and surface

The surface on a good rod guide must be of a hard and tight material. The guide material must be able to be polished to a very smooth surface to minimize friction to the line. It must also be sufficiently wear-resistant for the surface of the guide to remain unchanged when the line is pulled through backwards and forwards during the thousands of casts you make with a rod during its lifetime.

Bridge guides are a classic type of guide that in the past were common on fly rods and other light rods. Bridge guides consist of a chromed line guide soldered in a two-footed keeper – sometimes the keeper has support legs. After the ceramic guides made their entrance the bridge guide has almost disappeared. This is a pity, since it was a light and flexible guide that had both stability and height and was therefore a better alternative to snake guides for fly rods, and sometime to ceramic guides on UL rods.

Snake guides have been around for a long time and are still the most common on fly rods. The guides are manufactured in rather thin, i.e. metal wire, and since they are stretched as a

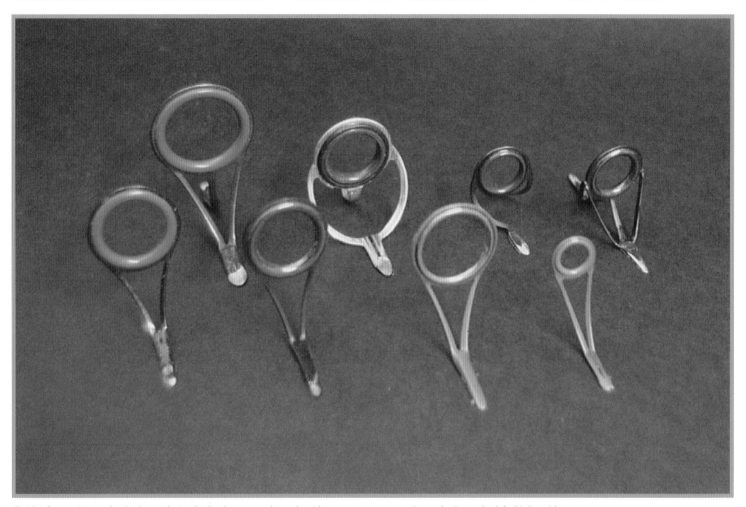

Guides for casting and spinning rods. In the back row two-legged guides – common on casting rods. From the left: high guide without support leg, low guide of standard model, guide with a so-called snake keeper and two-legged guide with support leg. In the foreground single leg guides for spinning rods, first three with standard keeper, the left with ceramic of standard quality, and a SIC guide and one of Gold Cermet. To the far right a guide with an extra high keeper.

"spiral" along the length they are very stable and yet remain flexible. Their big disadvantage is that they are extremely low, which leads to friction against the rod blank. A distinction is made between the American type, which are turned clockwise, and the English snake guides, which are turned anticlockwise.

Some time ago one-footed snake guides were a big innovation for fly rods, mainly in view of the fact that they had a one-footed, very light guide and in other words only needed one wrap per guide. In principle there is, however, no justification whatsoever for a one-footed snake guide, since the guide is still just as low as a normal snake guide, which furthermore was in fact flexible and required such short wraps

that one or two wraps would hardly have any noticeable difference on the action of the whole rod. But the guides soon become popular and ended up on quite a number of rods, both on home-made and mass produced rods.

Shortly afterwards high, one-footed snake guides turned up on the market, and then there was suddenly a point to having one-footed snake guides, since these in comparison with normal snake guides hold the line away from the blank and reduce the friction to it, as discussed above.

Nevertheless quite soon even this proved to be totally wrong. Because the high one-footed snake guides lack stability in the lengthwise direction of the blank, they have a large tendency to give way when exposed to strain. A knot on the line, something that happens occasionally when using monofilament line, that fastens in a guide can cause the guide to bend over.

It is quite simply not possible to manufacture a one-footed snake guide with the same stability as a two-footed guide, and if you add on the fact that they do not provide the rod with anything that produces better performance then as far as rod crafting is concerned they are of little interest. If the wire in the guides had been able to be made sufficiently strong to give the high guides the stability they needed if would have been different. The latter naturally applies to all rod guides – the keepers must be sufficiently stable to prevent deformation during the strain and stress produced by the fish.

Snake guides and bridge guides are usually chromed, and chrome is available in different qualities. The best, i.e. the hardest, is the so-called industrial chrome. Inspect the finish carefully – the chrome should be smooth and bright. Irregularities and matt sections are a result of poor preparation and finish and result in the line being braked and worn. In recent years coatings of titanium carbide (TIC, TiC, TiCh etc.) and titanium nitride (TIN, Ti.N, TiGold) have appeared, which are even harder than the chrome.

Titanium nitride is 50 % harder than the highest quality of industrial chrome. A titanium nitride coated rod guide is practically impossible to wear out and also has lower surface friction than one coated with normal chrome. Snake guides coated with titanium nitride and titanium carbide have now become common and are not much more expensive than chromed guides. But it is important to watch out when buying guides. There are also anodized snake guides which can easily be confused with them, but which have a surface coating that is far more softer then even inferior chrome.

Ceramic guides

Ceramic guides are manufactured in many different models and materials. The main construction, however, remains the same and an inner guide of a hard ceramic material is mounted in a metal keeper, sometimes with a shock-absorbing rubber ring in-between. Rod guide ceramics are always based on some type of hard chemical compound and the characteristics such as the ceramic's hardness, brittleness, polishability and heat conducting characteristics are determined by which chemical base the ceramic is manufactured of. The most important feature of ceramic guides, however, is always their height.

Since ceramic guides consist of two parts, sometimes three, they have a high mass and must be used with care. On light, slow rods a heavy set of ceramic guides can completely ruin the action. Most fast fly rods in the medium class and upwards, including casting and spinning rods, can however be fitted with ceramic guides without problem. One compromise that often functions is to use one-footed ceramic guides at the bottom of the rod and go over to another, lighter guide, e.g. snake guides, when you come up to the more pliant top section. The line guide and top ring should always be ceramic. Most of the better ceramic types of guides now have titanium keepers.

The fact that aluminum oxide is a hard material has been mentioned in the section on reel seats, and ceramics based on aluminum oxide have long been used for rod guides. Most usable rod guide ceramics in the medium-price class, e.g. Fuji's "green guides", are based on aluminum oxide. Aluminum oxide ceramics have low friction and withstand quite a lot of wear, but they can crack from knocks and blows. Aluminum oxide is available with different degrees of hardness, among other things depending on the purity of the material.

Other substances can also be used for rod guide ceramics, and depending on how hard they are the ceramic insets achieve different degrees of hardness. Titanium oxide and silicon carbide are common substances in rod guide ceramics. Silicon carbine ceramic (SIC, and Si.C etc. depending on the make, from Silicon Carbide, chemical symbol SiC) is one of the hardest available and is used for rod guides in the absolutely top class. It is dense, i.e. can be polished to achieve a very low friction, has a high resistance to wear, and leads off heat very well.

One disadvantage is that the harder the ceramic is, the more brittle the material becomes. SIC guides crack easily when exposed to knocks and blows, and you should check these types of rod guides often. A simple way of doing this is to pull a nylon stocking backwards and forwards through the guide a few times. If there are any cracks the thin nylon material will fasten in them.

Fuji manufactures a type of rod guide called Gold Cermet. This is a purely ceramic guide, but so similar in its structure that I include it here. The guide keeper is of the same type as on ceramic guides, but there is a combination guide on the keeper instead, ceramic coated with titanium nitride (TiN – the hard surface coating that replaces chrome on metal guides). The guides are lighter, stronger and more resistant to impact than SiC, and they can also be polished much smoother than SiC.

Tools and other materials

Most of the tools needed to build a rod can be found in a normal toolbox.

The best saw is a fine-toothed hacksaw and this gives the smoothest cutting surfaces and does not split the material as much as a rougher saw. It can also saw metal, which is necessary when modifying a reel seat for example. If you have reason to cut rod blanks, e.g. during repairs or when you want to make your own ferrules, it is a good idea to use a really worn hacksaw blade. It is easier to saw a rod blank without the risk of the fibers splitting with one of these.

Files are will be needed on several occasions. A metal file is needed for example to adjust the feet on the rod guides. A round file is used to file up the inner hole in the grip and wooden parts, and a both a rasp and wood file are needed to shape cork and wood for grips and for reel seat inserts, etc.

Sandpaper or abrasive paper is needed in several different degrees of coarseness. I usually use rough paper with particle size 80 to roughly shape cork grips and then switch over to about 150, to finish off with 400-600 for a really smooth surface. Wet abrasive paper with a particle size of about 1000 works well if you want to get a good finish on wooden parts.

A sharp and good hobby knife with replaceable blanks is useful in many different situations. For wrapping work you will need a razor blank to cut the thread with, and a scalpel is even better if you can get hold of one.

A standard electric drill is something of a universal tool when shaping wooden and cork parts. It is the only necessary tool that is a little more expensive to acquire. The drill also functions as a lathe if you support it on a bench in some way. Bench attachments can be bought for most types of drills, but I managed for a long time with a normal vice clamped to the bench.

Various types of clamping tools are needed when things need to be secured. A couple of screw clamps and a few glue presses go a long way.

Measuring tools are often needed. A ruler and folding rule are used for example to measure out the positioning of guides and other things. A pair of sliding calipers is good to have when making grips and reel seats.

A hole saw is a small tool that you can put in the drill when you want to make a round hole somewhat larger than what you can do with a normal drill. It saws out a small round piece from the material you want to make the hole in, and the

Top: No advanced special tools are required to build a rod and the illustration shows basically all that is necessary. From left to right in approximate order: denatured spirit for washing, household paper, hacksaw, folding rule, epoxy adhesive, files, drill with drills, sanding materials, knives, drawing materials and some other small items such as paper clips, rubber bands and masking tape, a taped metal rod with washers and nuts, and clamps and glue clamps.

Bottom: Wooden rings hollowed with a hole saw, ready to be glued together to sections for reel seat inserts, or shaped and glued into the grip as decorations. Hole saws can be purchased in well-sorted hardware stores and are not very expensive.

sawn out piece has a center hole from the drill the hole saw was placed on. A hole saw is invaluable when making the raw material for trim rings in grips and reel seats, or for butts, or for connections between blank and grips, etc.

Home-made special tools

A number of special tools are also very useful. They are often not available in the shop, but you can make them yourself very cheaply.

A grip clamp is used to fix the grip when it is glued to the rod. It consists of a pair of threaded metal rods, two wooden pads and a few nuts and washers. Drill a hole in one of the wooden pads so that it can be slipped over the rod down to the upper end of the grip (this is done before you have started mounting the rings). The other wooden pad supports the rod butt from underneath. Another hole is drilled on both sides of the hole for the rod blank in the upper pad, and the same is done on the corresponding place in the lower pad. The threaded rods are slipped through these, which with a pair of nuts in each end are used to pull the pads together so that the grip parts are pressed together on the rod. A few washers simplify things, and if you use wing nuts you will not need a tool to tighten with.

Threaded metal rods can be bought in your hardware store for a few dollars and they can also be used as a clamp when gluing and turning loose grip and reel seat parts. When, for example, gluing cork rings to the rod grip the rings are slipped up on a sufficiently thick threaded rod and pressed against each other by tightening with the nuts from both sides. When the grip is to be turned you place the whole package, the threaded rod and the rest, in the drill or the lathe.

A wrapping stand makes things easier when wrapping tight the rod guides. This is a cradle which the rod rests on horizontally when wrapping. A fully functioning wrapping stand

Above: A rod lathe is not a must, but is practical to have if you are building lots of rods. The illustration shows my home-made rod lathe. The box has recesses for the moveable reel supports, and the motor is a sewing machine motor. Everything is built of wood and the rollers are furniture castors from the nearest hardware store. The rod is mounted directly on the motor shaft with tape or an expanding rubber plug inside the end of the rod.

Below: A grip clamp is used to press the grip parts together on the blank while the glue is setting. The clamp is made of two wooden pads, one of them with a hole for the blank. The pads are pressed together by means of two through threaded rods, washers and nuts.

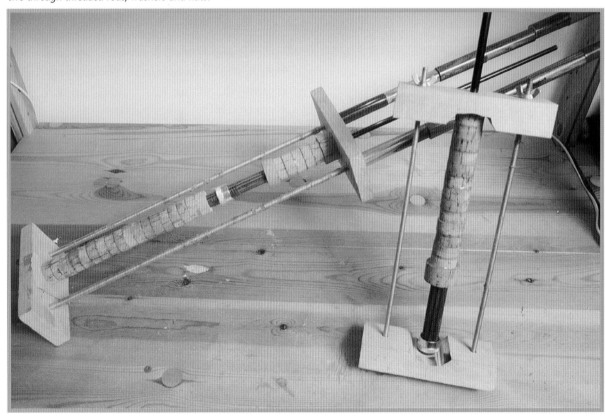

Different rod wrapping racks and in the background a drying arrangement for rod lacquer made from a battery operated grill motor. The rollers are wheels from model aircraft and the racks without rollers are covered with felt. The telephone directory functions as a wire tensioning device in that the thread goes through it and is tensioned by the friction to the pages. The bobbin of thread is placed in a tin can on the other side of the directory.

can be made from a pair of plastic bookends. File up a suitable notch in the top edge of the support and cover with felt to protect the blank from scratches. The support is fixed to the tabletop with a couple of clips or clamps.

A curing motor is a useful thing to have when lacquering rods, you then avoid having to rotate it by hand the first 3-4 minutes until the lacquer has stopped running. A battery-powered grill motor can be bought in a hardware store for very little and functions quite satisfactorily. The motor can be mounted by way of suggestion in a similar book support as the one you used for the wrapping support, and used together with it, so that the rod rests and rotates horizontally during the curing. The rod blank is protected from wear with a few pieces of tape where it rubs against the wrapping supports.

Glue

Glue for building fishing rods must not age. If the glue looses its properties in the course of time the joints will release,

something which is guaranteed to happen just when you are playing a large fish, or at some other inappropriate moment. Apart from that the reel seat and grip seldom fit perfectly to the blank, and therefore the glue has two purposes – to joint the parts to together, and as a filler to fill out the cavities between the blank and the components placed on it so that the joint becomes solid. For this reason the glue must never shrink either when it cures.

All "normal" glues that dry through the evaporation of the solvent are completely out of the question. Firstly they shrink during the evaporation, and secondly the ventilation under a fishing rod grip is not good enough, which means that this type of glue never dries. A glue for building fishing rods must cure chemically, i.e. through the reaction of different chemical substances to each other, and therefore two-component glues are the only ones that are a possible choice.

Epoxy is actually the only possible choice, it fills out well, cures through a chemical reaction (not evaporation), and its

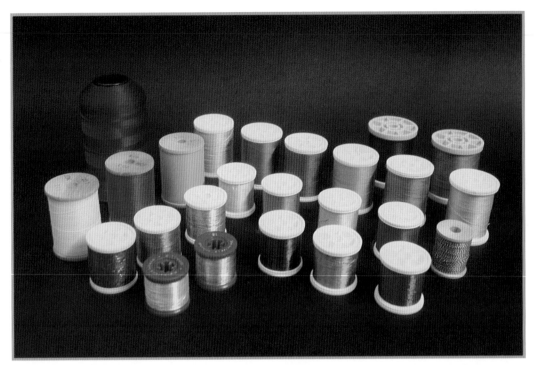

Wrap threads of different types. To the left in the background a bulk spool. In front of it three bobbins of thread of the NCP type (No Color Preserver), which retain their color without color preserver. This thread is duller in color than normal thread. The two rows of metallic thread in front of these are sewing thread of the metallic type, which as opposed to other common sewing thread functions excellently. To the right more standard thread on different sizes of spools, and to the front three spools of metallic rod wrapping thread.

volume remains constant during the curing – no cavities are formed. But there are different types of epoxies on the market, and it is important that it is the right kind of epoxy.

The so-called fast glues, 5-minute epoxy, fast epoxy or whatever they are called, that cure in a few minutes or up to an hour, are clearly not suitable. Firstly they cure so quickly that it would be difficult to manage to get all the parts in place, and if you are in a hurry when you are gluing it can easily happen that you put some component in the wrong place. If the glue has then cured it will not be possible to remove the incorrectly positioned part from the rod again without either destroying it or sawing into the blank. Moreover, when gluing you have to manage to clean all the surfaces from any smeared glue and put the parts in a press so that the joints become tight.

Another property that makes fast epoxies unsuitable is that in the course of time they become hard and brittle, which means they cannot follow the movements of the rod – the glue cracks and rod parts come loose. Since a rod is flexible, a glue for building rods must be, and remain, elastic. Epoxy with a long curing time, approximately one day, has this property and there are a small number of such these on the market.

5-minute epoxy does function well in one stage, it is excellent to fasten the top ring. If it should later need to be changed, you just warm the joint over a flame to release it. Hot-set epoxy also functions well for the top ring.

Cork should not be glued with epoxy. Cork is an elastic and soft material that is also very easy to grind, and if you glue together cork rings with epoxy, which becomes hard after curing), you can get hard "edges" or rings in the grip when you shape it. You can feel these rings when holding the grip and it is annoying. Furthermore, because of the hardness of the glue it can be difficult to shape a regular grip with a good finish in the surface. When gluing cork rings together, for example for grip materials, you should use contact glue.

Thread

Thread for rod wraps should be pliant, have long fibers (no fluff) and not be too slippery. The strength is less important, even a very small rod guide is pressed to the blank by at least some 50 turns of thread, and their collective pressure will be sufficient even if the thread is not particularly tightly wrapped. The thread also shrinks during the lacquering, which increases the pressure round the ring foot. A thin-walled blank can even become deformed from a too tightly wrapped thread, which can lead to the rod breaking or a compressed female ferrule.

The best thread has always been manufactured by the American Gudebrod. Sewing thread and other similar thread are short-fibred, which means that the wraps become fluffed, i.e. cannot be used. On the other hand it is possible to use the different types of metallic sewing thread that are available for decorative purposes.

Lacquer

When the wraps on the rod are coated you will need two lacquers. First of all you will need a primer, a so-called color preserver. This has several purposes, it preserves as the name implies the color of the wrapping thread so that the wrap retains the appearance you created when you made it. Color preserver also causes the wrapping thread to contract, which means that the wrap "tightens" round the guide foot and makes the guide sit more securely. The color preserver also fills up all the possible cavities in the wrap. If these contain air when you apply the surface lacquer there will be a tendency for bubbles to form, resulting in the wrap having a poor finish.

On top of the color preserver you then apply surface lacquer, which produces a strong and wear-resistant surface and a gloss finish for the wrap. Two-component polymer or epoxy lacquers produce bright, transparent surfaces that never yellow with age. There are also water-based rod lacquers that produce a good finish, although they require rather a large number of coats, and there are varnish-like rod lacquers. The latter are not to be recommended because just like all varnishes they turn yellow with age. Most polymer lacquers are unfortunately somewhat viscous, and the lacquering can easily become clumsy. A rod where each wrapping looks like a small pearl is not only aesthetically annoying, the rod also becomes burdened by an increase in its inherent mass from the lacquer. So it is a question of keeping the coats as thin as possible. If you have the opportunity to choose, use the thinnest polymer lacquer possible.

Sometimes you see rod building descriptions that recommend lacquering the wraps with only surface lacquer, without pretreatment with color preserver. The motivation for this differs but is often rather diffuse, to the effect that "it will be more subdued, only one lacquer is needed and this makes the crafting more Spartan", or something similar. For several tangible reasons this is not to be recommended. Rod lacquers have the characteristic that they make the rod wrapping thread transparent, which not only changes the color of the thread, but also means that you can see the blank and the guide foot through the wrap. All the light surfaces and marks in the guide foot after the adjustments you have made can be clearly seen, which can be annoying in an otherwise attractive and pure design.

Moreover, surface lacquer as opposed to color preserver has the characteristic that it causes the rod wrapping thread to stretch, which means that the wrap can release or move during the brushing. And since the thread does not tighten, the rod guide is only held in place by means of the lacquer quite simply "gluing" the guide foot to the blank. If you subsequently need to replace a guide on some occasion this can be a problem. Lacquer that lies on color preserver releases without problem if you need to remove it, but lacquer in contact with a rod blank is difficult to remove, and often takes the surface layer of the blank with it. Neither has the lacquer any inherent strength against breaking forces, and cracks easily – the guide simply does not sit equally secure. After all it is the thread that is supposed to hold the guide to the rod.

Other good things

Masking tape is the rod crafter's universal tool number one and there are few stages in the construction of a rod where you cannot derive benefit from a roll of masking tape. It is needed to fill out under grip parts, to temporarily hold rod guides secure, to provide protection from glue, to hold the thread during decorative wraps, and to remove fluff from the surface of wraps – there is no end to its usefulness. Keep plenty of masking tape at home when building your rod.

Mentholated spirits or denatured alcohol is used for cleaning purposes after gluing with epoxy or lacquering with two-component lacquers. You need of course rags or household paper to wipe up with, and when cleaning inaccessible places a pipe cleaner drenched in spirits often solves the problem. After lacquering with two-component lacquer the brushes can be cleaned in spirits.

A tackcloth is used when painting cars but is also excellent to remove the last dust on a rod before you lacquer it. They are available from the paint shops and cost very little.

You will also need of course pen and paper, brushes and various types of things to solve temporary tasks and problems, such as rubber bands, paper clips and the like.

Preparations

Start the actual crafting by making a sketch.

Before you start building the rod grip it is a good idea to plan the project thoroughly. Carefully think through what you want the rod to be like, what the grip and reel seat should look like and their size, measure up all the parts carefully, measure the length of the reel foot, and make a sketch on paper. A regular drawing is not necessary, but an explicit sketch where all the shapes and sizes are indicated is an invaluable help when you going to shape the grip and fit it together with the reel seat. Meanwhile you will also have the opportunity to think through the technical details and in which order things should be done. This is a good idea if you prefer not to be left standing there later on with a pair of glued rod parts, suddenly realizing that the whole thing is not going to function as you had thought.

Think through how the rod is to be used and take into consideration both external factors and your own characteristics – arms, hands, how you hold a rod, and all the other personal factors that can play a role in how you design the rod. The rod should fit well in your hand, and it should feel secure and comfortable. A few moments in front of the rod rack in the fishing tackle shop with a few

different rods is time well spent. Simulate different fishing situations as far as possible, "cast" and "play" etc. in the way you would do in reality. All conceivable factors, even the weather and the season the rod is going to be used in play a part. For example on a spinning rod for fishing sea trout in winter conditions it is a good idea to shape the reel seat so as to minimize the metal surfaces the hand comes into contact with when you are holding the rod.

It is also important not to let yourself be bound to the shapes and dimensions common on commercial rods. Traditional thinking is a common handicap of rod manufacturers and rod buyers, and there is not much innovative rod designing among the mass producers. If you have the ability to see an issue without blinkers and think along new lines there are almost always new solutions to both old and new problems. This is important, because the rod we are going to build will as we know be unique and the actual reason why we are building it ourselves is because we want to achieve something that cannot be bought.

When you are reasonably clear about your design you make your sketch, as far as possible complete with the specified measurements of all the sizes, lengths and other dimensions. Draw cross-sections of all the connections between different parts. Check the reel seat and blank etc. so that everything agrees, and so that the rod parts will fit where you want to have them.

An explicit sketch indicating all the dimensions and shapes simplifies things when constructing the grip.
Once the sketch has been drawn you have the opportunity to think through all the details.

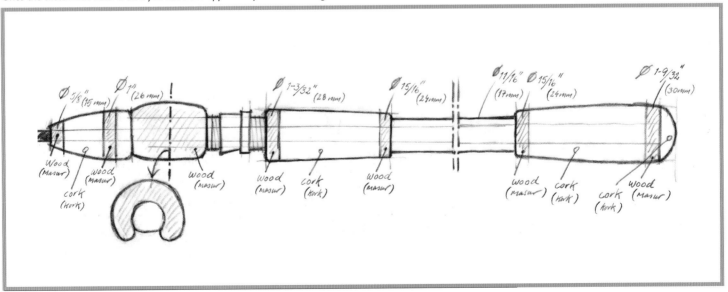

Wrapping the ferrules

All the ferrules must be wrapped and the wraps treated with color preserver before it is possible to do anything else with rod blank! Never put together an unwrapped rod ferrule. The material in graphite blanks has almost no strength to resist cracking or compressive forces since in principle all the reinforcing graphite fibers go along the length. This cannot be overemphasized and there are probably quite a few prospective rod crafters who have disconcertedly had to confirm that the ferrule cracked before they had even started the work.

It is the female ferrule that has to be wrapped and this must be done along its entire length. It serves no purpose as on certain rods to limit the wrapping to just a short wrap at the far end and perhaps a short wrap at the beginning of the ferrule. When the rod is put together the cracking force can occur at any point along the ferrule. Sometimes you can determine from the shape of the ferrules how far in the male ferrule goes, sometimes you have to test it by very carefully bringing the blank parts together – not pressing them together – and mak-

ing a mark. Add on a few millimeters so that the whole of the ferrule length is guaranteed to be wrapped, and wrap over the full distance with rod wrapping thread, which should be immediately treated with color preserver.

On most rods apart from the very lightest it is a good idea to wrap the ferrule double at the far end. Start the wrapping at the beginning of the ferrule, a few millimeters inside the point where the male ferrule reaches during assembly, and wrap out towards the outer end of the ferrule. Here you work back and wrap another half to one centimeter over the first layer of thread, after which the wrapping is finished. More about wrapping techniques further on.

Do not pull the thread too hard, on thin-walled blanks the wrapping can "compress the material", which can lead to a poor fit. How hard the thread should be stretched is difficult to say. Some form of "normal tension" should be applied, where the thread lies safety in place without being stretched too much. The color preserver used to treat the thread before the ferrules are put together also further tightens the threads.

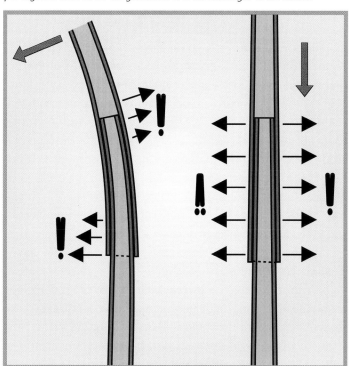

Cracking forces in the rod ferrule. Forces are generated in the ends of the ferrule when the rod is bent, which can crack it if it is not reinforced. When the rod is put together such forces are generated over the full length of the ferrule.

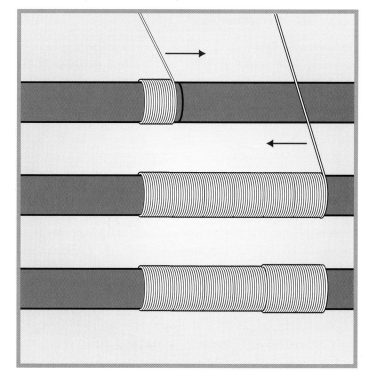

The ferrule should be wrapped along its entire length before it is put together. On heavier rods you turn round at the outer end of the ferrule and wrap back a little, so that you have a double layer of thread there.

he different thickness of the walls in the blank cause spine effects. It can be clearly seen in the end of the ferrule that the walls on this rod blank have an unequal thickness on different sides. This photographed rod blank is one of the most expensive prestige brands.

Mark out the spine

Another necessary stage that must be done before the components can be mounted is to find out how the spine lies in the blank. In order to avoid any misunderstanding as we go along it is important for us to define the concept of the spine and clarify what we mean when talking about the spine side and its opposite, the "belly side", or what we are now going to call it.

Rod blanks are manufactured by wrapping a graphite cloth, drenched in a hot-setting epoxy bonding agent, round a tapering metal core. A foil is wound outside to hold it all in place, after which it allowed to cure in an oven. During the heating process the material that is to make up the blank becomes more or plastic, i.e. flexible, and under the influence of gravity and the pressure from the outer layer of foil the blank material can "wander" to a greater or lesser extent round the metal core. The result is that the finished walls of the blank have a slightly different material thickness on different sides, which in turn produce differences in the flexibility in different directions.

The spine can be more perceptible to a greater or lesser extent on different blanks, even if they belong to the same manufacturing series. In some cases there are even several "spines" on different sides of the blank as a result of the fact that several areas with a greater material thickness have developed, including intermediate sections with thinner blank walls. Rod blanks in the more expensive price classes are sometimes alleged to lack the spine effect as a result of the high precision used during the manufacturing process, but this is not true. The spine can be found on all types and price classes of blanks. Neither is the spine a problem, on the contrary if you can utilize the effects of the spine correctly when building the rod it becomes more of an advantage for the final result.

Test to find the spine sides

Prepare for the spine test by fastening a piece of masking tape round the blank, approximately in the middle, so that you have something to mark the spine sides when you find them. Now let the blank, you do this with each blank part separately, rest with its top end towards a stable support, e.g. the edge of a

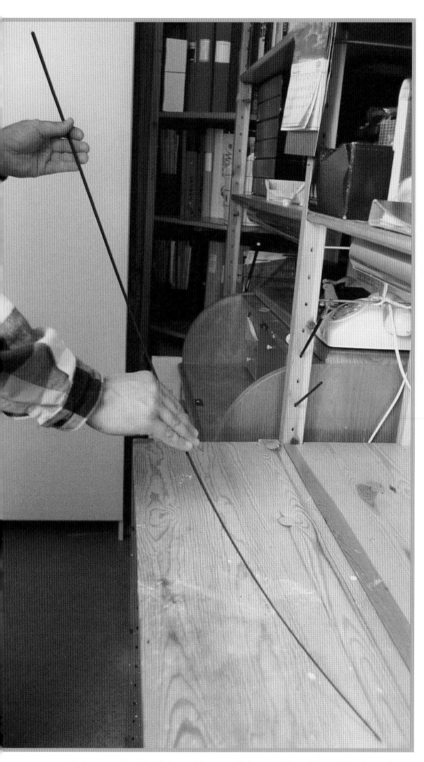

Spine test. The tip of the rod is pressed down to the table so that the rod bends. The right hand rolls it forwards and backwards to find the soft and hard sides.

table. You let the thicker end of the blank rest against the palm of your right hand, and you hold this hand rather high – the blank should slope down from your hand to the table that the top end is resting on at an angle of approximately 45 degrees. Use the thumb and forefinger of your left hand to grip the blank approximately in the middle and press it down towards the table so that it bends, and is well tensioned. Now roll it backwards and forwards between your thumb and forefinger.

The blank will want to remain in certain positions when you roll it during the bending. This is because it is smoother in that direction and wants to bend to it. In other positions it is the reverse, the blank provides more resistance to the bending that occurs now than in the other direction. The result is that it makes a slight "jump" over this position and wants to roll on to one of the other rest positions.

Try to find the bending direction that gives the most resistance, i.e. in the middle of the above mentioned "jump", and mark the side that is then facing upwards (i.e. the side in which direction the blank bends when it makes the most resistance) with a pencil mark on the masking tape. This side, the side in which direction the blank produces more resistance to bending that in the other directions, we call the spine side. As a rule the blank will have such a side, with a soft side or a "belly" which it would prefer to bend towards more or less opposite to it.

In certain cases the blank may have two or even more spine sides, and to complicate matters these may not even lie opposite to each other. If so you should mark both (all) of these. Try also to determine if one of these "spines" is stronger than the others, and if so mark it separately.

Position of the spine

The spine governs which side of the blank the rod guides should be put on, and accordingly also how you mount the reel seat. Before mounting the grip and reel seat you therefore have to decide how the rod guides should be placed in relation to the spine. The orientation of the spine in the rod is important for its characteristics in several different ways. Above all it influences the casting length and the precision, but also the balance in the rod.

The blank is in other words stronger on different sides, which you can notice by the blank producing more resistance to being bent in different directions. When actually fishing the rod mainly works with bending actions directed straight

If the spine (red point) is positioned correctly (left cross-section) the casting movement will the straight. If it is positioned to the side of the rod's center line (right cross-section) this will result in torsion, which will make the casting movement curved and the line path irregular.

forward and straight backward in the direction of the cast. When positioning the guides, grip and reel seat, it is therefore important to make sure that the rod is not unequally strong on different sides of the casting direction. The whole thing is basically about achieving balance between the sides of the blank in the casting direction. The sides of the blank that have unequal strength must be placed "behind each other" – in the casting plane – otherwise they steal force and reduce the precision. The spine, if there is only one, is placed so that it lies either forwards or backwards in the casting plane. This choice is determined by which action you want the rod to have. If there are several "spines" you position these so that there will be equal strength on both sides of the casting plane.

If for example you are going to build the rod so that the strongest side of the blank lies to the right of the casting plane, then the right side of the blank will produce greater resistance to bending than the left when it is working forwards and backwards during the fishing. The strong side to the left produces greater resistance to the bending, the weak side to the left follows easily along when the rod bends. This will mean that the blank turns slightly when you bend it, in one direction when it bends backwards, and in the other when it is bent forwards in the casting direction. The tip of the rod will not move straight forwards or backwards, but rather describe a curved motion.

You can notice this in that the rod feels unbalanced, in that it is "unsettling" to cast with so that you have to concentrate on the casting, above all the casting direction, more than you are used to. The precision can also be affected and since the tip of the rod has a tendency to swing sideways it will not cast out the bait or the line exactly in the direction you directed the cast. If it is a fly rod these side swings can give rise to vibrations in the line, which can have an adverse effect on the casting length.

Spine and casting length

Casting with casting and spinning rods works by means of the cast weight you shoot out pulling the line after it, and the casting length is determined above all by the force you can put behind the cast mass just in the moment of casting. A number of other factor also play a large role of course, such as the braking effect of the line, the aerodynamic properties of the bait, and the angle of the cast trajectory, etc. You can influence some of these while building the rod because they are related to the actual design of the rod, and the first one of them is the

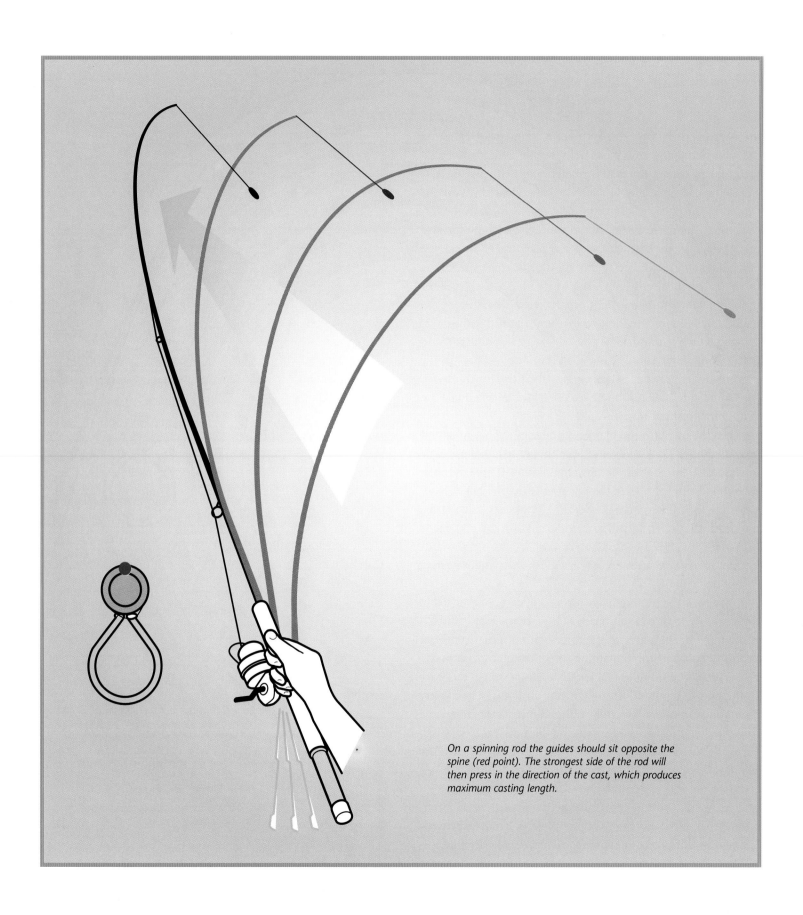

On a spinning rod the guides should sit opposite the spine (red point). The strongest side of the rod will then press in the direction of the cast, which produces maximum casting length.

force in the cast. You influence this by correctly positioning the spine on the rod in relation to the casting direction.

A rod functions approximately like a steel spring or a trampoline in the cast action. You charge it with a movement in the opposite direction, a backward cast. In the case of a spring or a trampoline the force it can deliver depends on how much force it has been compressed or deflected with before it is released – it accumulates force that is later released. The rod is loaded in the backward cast and delivers the force in the forward cast. The more force the rod can deliver in the forward cast, the longer the cast will be. If you place the grip, reel seat and guides so that the rod is bent towards its spine side in the forward cast, in the direction in which the blank produces most resistance to being bent, then the hardest side of the blank will press in the forward cast and the rod can be discharged to a maximum. The rod will work fast and you will cast a long way. This means that the side we had facing upwards when we did the above described test for the spine, the "spine side", should be directed backwards when you are casting in a normal way with rod.

If instead you turn the blank 180 degrees so that its softest side is directed backwards and accordingly works during the forward cast, the rod will be slower and not cast as far. On the other hand you can utilize the full strength of the blank in all situations where it is arced forwards – hook fish, and lift the line from the water. In other words you place the spine side backwards if you want to achieve casting length, and forwards if you want to have strength for playing fish and handling heavy bait or lines.

In fly rods the prerequisites for a long cast are somewhat different. The bait in itself has very little mass, and instead it is the mass of the line and the force behind it that pulls out both the bait and the remaining line. Since the mass of the line is extended along its full length you have to get the force of the cast to "wander" along the line all the way to its very end. You do not achieve this in the first instance by a large force, rather through a distinct and definite "stop", which stops the forward cast and effectively transfers the force the blank is loaded with in the backward cast to the line.

When the rod is stopped in the forward cast this creates a line arc, a "fold" or a bend in the line where the forward directed line that goes out from the tip of the rod, bends backwards in the direction to the remaining line, leader and fly that it is pulling after it. The line arc should wander forwards along the

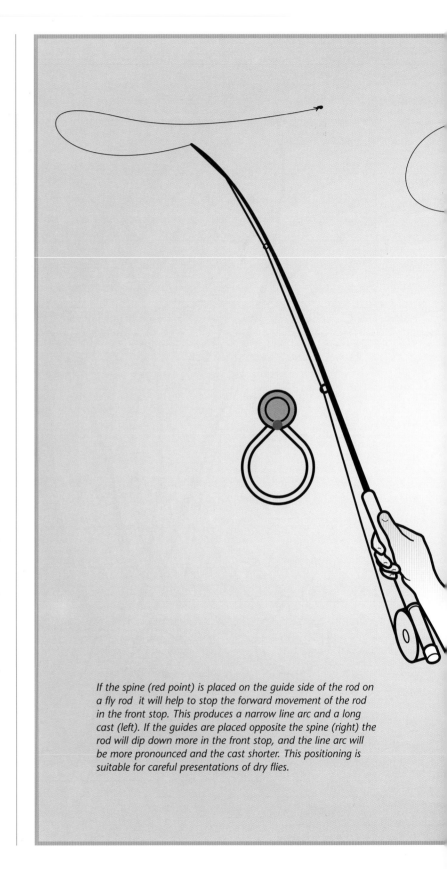

If the spine (red point) is placed on the guide side of the rod on a fly rod it will help to stop the forward movement of the rod in the front stop. This produces a narrow line arc and a long cast (left). If the guides are placed opposite the spine (right) the rod will dip down more in the front stop, and the line arc will be more pronounced and the cast shorter. This positioning is suitable for careful presentations of dry flies.

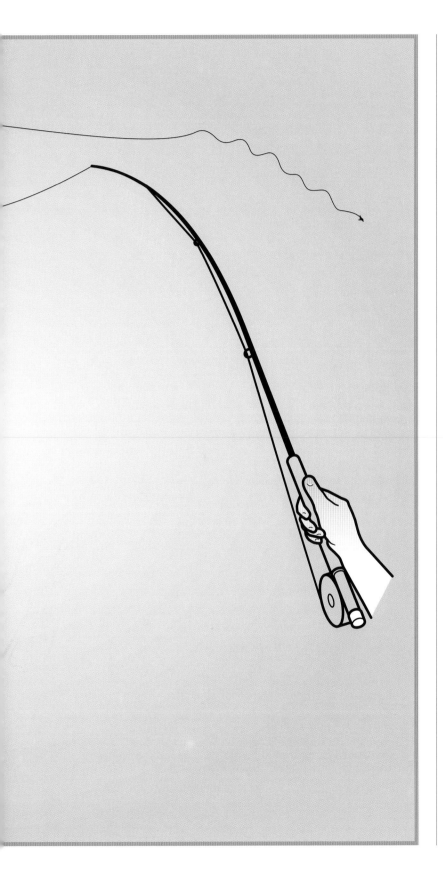

entire line until is straightens out the leader and finally delivers the fly in the water in the extension of the leader. You could say that it is precisely in the line arc that the wandering force in the cast is concentrated. The line arc is braked by the air resistance and the greater the area it offers the air to influence it, the greater the braking effect. In other words a large line arc is braked significantly more than a small one.

When a rod has been stopped in the forward cast it still functions as a trampoline. The trampoline strikes up when the jumper has left it and then stands and vibrates for a while. The tip of the rod strikes forwards, it "dips". How far it strikes downwards-forwards is important for the size of the line arc – small dipping, small line arc. The vibrations that come after the dip are also dampened if the first dip was not too large. In other words it is good for the casting length to place the spine in a fly rod so that it dampens the dipping of the rod forwards-downwards as much as possible. You achieve this by mounting the grip, reel seat and guides so that the rod has the spine side forwards-downwards when you are casting with it in a normal way.

Multiple spines

If the rod blank has two spines opposite to each other you can choose been placing the spine plane or the soft side plane (90 degrees to the spine plane) in the casting direction. The first produces a fast action – the tip of the rod stops quickly. If you place the soft sides in the casting plane this produces a slower action and larger line arc, but on the other hand reduces the tendency of the rod to swing sideways. It produces a more balanced feeling and the rod becomes more comfortable to cast with. Precision rods should have this kind of guide positioning, and it also works well for light fly rods when the presentation is more important than the casting length.

A blank with two spines does not always have them positioned exactly opposite each other. In this case the blank will roll more than a half turn between the two positions where you can feel the spine sides when testing the blank. If you continue the turn there will be less than a half turn left before you feel that you are back to the first spine side. The soft side, between the spine sides, that is longer than a half turn is called the long soft side. The other, the opposite side, that is less that a half turn is the short side. The short soft side is in general stiffer than the long.

On this type of blank it is not possible to place one of the spine sides in the casting plane. It would result in the other,

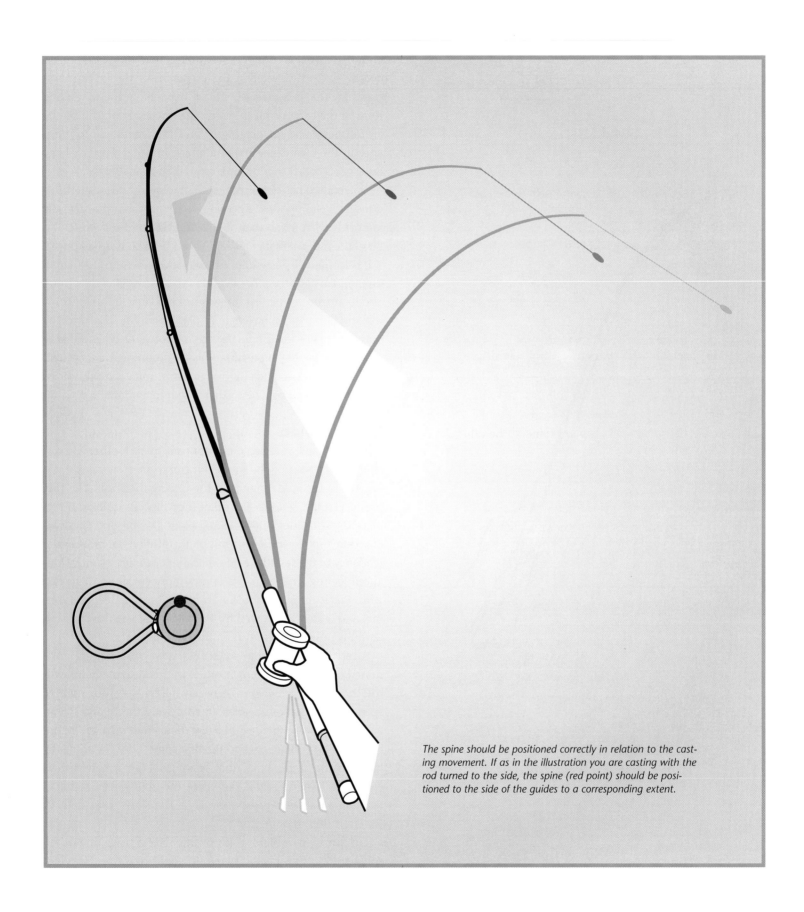

The spine should be positioned correctly in relation to the casting movement. If as in the illustration you are casting with the rod turned to the side, the spine (red point) should be positioned to the side of the guides to a corresponding extent.

not quite opposite spine side, ending up to the side of the casting plane in one or the other direction. This situation would produce instability sideways, cause the line to be braked and result in inferior precision, see above. You must place the spine sides equidistant to the side of the casting plane in both directions, and consequently one of the soft side must end up forwards in the casting plane.

If you place the short soft side backwards in the casting direction the rod will produce the best possible forward action in the cast, and in other words you will have the pre-requisites for long casts with casting and spinning rods. On fly rods, according to the above reasoning about blanks with one spine, the tip of the rod will dip less in the forward cast and produce narrower line arcs, if you place the short soft side forwards in the casting plane, which produces long casts.

Note that all these guidelines for the positioning of the spine in the rod are based on the casting direction or casting plane, the "slice of air" the blank cuts through forwards and backwards during a cast. Nevertheless it is not self-explanatory that the rod guides should be placed exactly on, or exactly opposite the spine. Many people turn the rod in one or the other direction when they are casting. Often unconsciously, but some-times deliberately and with a definite purpose. For example, some people mean that you should turn the reel out from the body when casting with a fly rod. Another example is casting with level-wind reels, a subject I intend to devote a few lines to.

Casting techniques with casting rods vary enormously and this influences the positioning of the guides. Some people cast the reel horizontally on the top side of the reel as an enclosed single-action reel, in which case the spine should be directed backwards and the guides placed on the rod's spine side.

But the "correct" technique that the level-wind reel is made for is with the rod turned 90 degrees so that the reel in the outward cast "stands on its end" on the side of the rod where you have the thumb of the casting hand. A fisherman who casts with the right hand should therefore have the reel turned 90 degrees to the left when casting (see sketch). The reason for this is rather intricate, but if you think about it quite logical.

If you cast with the reel straight up on the rod then the thumb on the casting hand plays the biggest role in the trans-mission of force between hand and rod. It is the thumb you "apply the pressure" with in the cast. But at the same time it is precisely the thumb that should release the button or the line spool at the critical moment. And at the same time as you apply most pressure! It is also the same thumb that should control the delivery of the line from the spool to prevent the line from rising. It speaks for itself that such a casting tech-nique produces poor control and precision.

If on the other hand you turn the rod the previously-men-tioned 90 degrees the thumb suddenly looses it entire role in the transmission of power. Instead, the base of the forefinger and inside of the hand take up the most force and apply pressure on the rod in the forward cast. And voilá! The thumb is now free to release, brake the spool, and adjust exactly as you want it. The control, casting length and precision increase dramatically. Try it yourself if you do not believe me, I promise you it works.

But it is still the spine side that should be directed back-wards in the casting plane if you want to fully utilize the strength of the blank. In other words the guides should, if you adopt the casting technique described above, not sit in the spine plane but 90 degrees to the side on a casting rod, so that it is precisely the spine that is directed backwards during the forward cast. For most people the final casting technique will be something in-between, in which case you adapt yourself to this and position the guides accordingly. It is always the spine that should be directed straight backwards.

It is important to understand how you turn the rod in relation to the casting plane when you are casting. If you do it in one of the above ways or have the rod turned in some other way, the spine should preferably be correctly orientated in relation to the casting action, which means that you mount the guides, grip and reel seat more less at an angle in relation to this.

When you are clear about all this you wrap new tape on the blank and mark on each blank part the side the reel and guides should be placed on. Remove all the old spine mark-ings to avoid confusion later on.

Making a reel seat

The reel seat is a part of the grip construction on most rods and when you build your rod grip it is often a natural part of the working procedure to first shape the reel seat and then build it into the grip. We will begin by adjusting it to the reel.

The purpose of modifying a reel seat is first and foremost to minimize the metal surfaces. Metal is cold and uncomfortable to hold, and the reel foot does not sit well on a slippery metal surface. Since the reel seat should fulfill its function, hold the reel secure, but not replace the grip as a grip-

ping surface, it should also be just long enough so that you can put on and take off the reel, but no longer. The best thing is if you have the opportunity to build the rod for a special reel so that you can adjust the reel seat exactly to the length of the reel foot. But even if this is not the case, the rod is as a rule intended for a specific casting weight or line class. This limits the number of suitable reel sizes, and reel feet do not differ very much in the same category. If you cut the reel seat so that there is a half to one centimeter of extra space to the reel foot there is little risk of having problems if you change the reel later.

The reel seat is just long enough to allow the reel to be taken out when it is completely open.
This minimizes the size of the reel seat so that you can hold the cork instead of the metal.

Cutting

When cutting the reel seat it is important to avoid scratching the surface and to saw so that the edges are as clean and smooth as possible. You protect lacquer or anodizing with masking tape, which is wrapped a few turns directly over the place you are going to cut. Mark the sawing line all the way round the reel seat body over the masking tape, and saw through the tape and reel seat with a hacksaw. Do not saw all the way through from one side, stop instead as soon as the saw has gone through the material, turn the reel seat a little, and saw through again, and so on, until you have worked all the way round the reel seat and cut it. It is when sawing from one side to the other, and when the saw in the middle of the tube goes at right angles to the thin material, that there is a risk of it hacking and deforming the reel seat.

After this the edges should be sanded, without making the cut beveled or curved. The human machine is not made for linear movements and a forward and return sanding movement by hand easily becomes a curved movement, which produces uneven sanding pressure with a bent or beveled surface as a result. A special method is needed to get the sandpaper to work equally all round.

Place the sandpaper flat with the rough side up on a smooth surface such as a tabletop. Put a pencil mark on the edge of the reel seat and place it on the sandpaper, level on the cut surface and with the mark facing you. Hold the sandpaper firmly with one hand and pull the reel seat once towards you while holding it level against the sandpaper. Turn it slightly. Lift it up from the sandpaper, move it back and repeat the procedure – pull it towards you level along the sandpaper, once. Continue to turn and pull in this way until you have turned the reel seat a complete turn and the pencil mark is facing you again. In this way you can make sure that the sanding surface is level and that the sanding is applied equally around the edge of the reel

Top left: Protect the reel seat with masking tape when sawing. Saw in the middle of the tape. When the saw has gone through the material turn the reel seat slightly, and then saw through the material again. Continue in this way all round.

Bottom left: Sand the cut surface by pulling it along a piece of sandpaper lying flat on a table. Turn the reel seat slightly between each pull.

seat. Check that the surface has become completely flat, and if not repeat the procedure.

The same facing technique is used for cut grip pieces, wooden inserts and blanks etc. and the method of turning a little between each file stroke is also used when fitting blank parts into each other, or to file up the inner diameter of a grip so that it fits the blank. The slight turn between the file strokes reduces any effects of holding it at an angle and guarantees that the sanding is done equally in all directions, so that the inner hole of the cork ring or grip remains in the middle.

When you have gone round one turn you have cut an equal amount on all sides.

Making a reel seat insert

If you want to go one step further with the modification you can try replacing all unnecessary metal or plastic surfaces in the reel seat body with another materials. The only part that must remain is of course the actual thread, and only enough of it that is needed for the length of the reel foot. The rest of the reel seat body can in other words be replaced with, for example, cork.

Use the reel foot as a template and measure up how long the thread needs to be, it should permit the lock nut and lock sleeve to move enough for the reel to be able to be taken off and put on, but not more. Mark and saw – saw off the reel seat body just up to the house cap. The piece the house cap sits on should be left on. Cork is soft and becomes pressed together if you put the house cap directly on a cork cylinder without a supporting under layer for the reel foot.

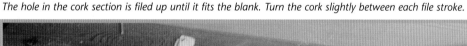

The hole in the cork section is filed up until it fits the blank. Turn the cork slightly between each file stroke.

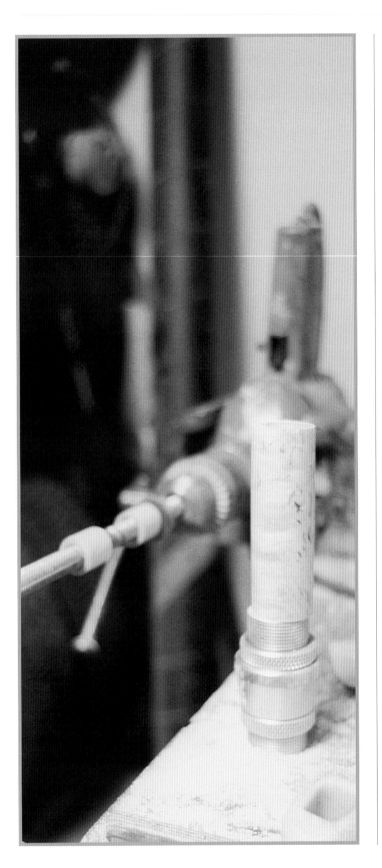

Finished reel seat insert. In the background the drill it was turned in, with tape built up on the threaded rod in the drill chuck.

Glue together a cork section from two to three sufficiently large cork rings. If the reel seat insert is to be made of wood you cut the piece of wood you intend to use instead and drill up a hole through the length of it. Remember that both the part of the reel seat body that is to be used as thread and the one that the house cap sits on should be slipped up and glued on the ends of the reel seat insert, and therefore the length of the section must be sufficient for this too.

The hole in the raw section should be big enough for the thickness of the blank where the reel seat is to sit. If for example the holes in the cork rings are too small you file them up to an adequate size. Use the technique described above, one stroke with the file, a slight turn of the section, and one stroke etc. to keep the hole round and in the middle of the cork.

After this the section is threaded up on a threaded metal rod with the help of washers and nuts on both ends. It is not necessary to have access to a proper lathe to be able to make a reel seat insert of wood, a drill and a few files will go a long way. The technique you use is the same as when making trim rings and turning rod grips.

The threaded rod is placed in the chuck of the drill, which is fixed to the edge of the table with some form of holder. The section is turned down to the required shape by means of files and sandpaper. Make the cork cylinder slightly thicker than the reel seat so that the reel foot will tension slightly and sit more securely. Grind down the cylinder in both ends so that the thread and house cap can be slipped on and sit firmly. To achieve the sharp edges needed where the thread and house cap are to connect you can use a hacksaw and hold it against the turning section. Finally, you remove the finished reel seat insert from the threaded rod and glue on the reel seat parts in both ends.

Wooden rings and other materials

Turned sections of wood can be made from wooden rings taken out with a hole saw. If you saw the rings out of a slab of wood you will have sections ready with center holes for check rings, butts and effect rings. 5-10 rings can be glued together to form a section for a reel seat insert. The fact that it is not made of one piece of wood is not a disadvantage, on the contrary, by combining rings of different species of

Cork and wooden rings are glued together to one piece on a threaded rod. If the rod is too thin its diameter can be built up with tape.

wood and setting the grain in different directions you can create very interesting effects.

Wooden rings are glued together with slow curing epoxy, while cork rings are glued with contact glue. Drill or file up the rings so that they can be slipped on the blank down to the place where the reel seat is to sit. It does not really matter if the holes are slightly askew since the turning will center them again.

If the threaded rod is narrower than the inner holes of the rings they will fit loosely on the rod. You then fill up the intervening space with hard-rolled "bushings" of masking tape until they sit firmly. Do not wrap tape round the stretch of the threaded rod that is to be covered! This will produce an irregular and out of center filling, which the section will not sit properly on. The reason we use the threaded rod during the gluing is so that all the inner holes will come exactly in line. It is also used as a holder during the turning, since in this way we can get the hole to end up in the middle of the ready-turned insert. For this to work the threaded rod must be held exactly in the middle of the tape filling and it must form a hard, smooth cylinder. Put tape on the threaded rod in hard

rolls beside each other until the space is completely filled, but make the filling a few millimeters short so that it can be pressed together during the gluing.

Apply glue to the flat surfaces of the rings. Make sure that no glue gets into their inner holes, otherwise they will be glued to the threaded rod. Bear in mind that glue can creep in when you press the rings together. Epoxy is applied thinly on only one surface of the wooden ring and you leave a few millimeters free by the hole. Contact glue is used when gluing cork, and this should be applied on both of the surfaces. You should also allow it to dry until the glue is no longer sticky before you bring the surfaces together. Think about the ventilation – contact glue contains thinner, which is dangerous for the nerve system, and the epoxies and amides emitted by epoxy adhesive are if possible even more dangerous, even if they do not smell equally strong.

When all the preparations have been made you bring the rings together on the threaded rod and put them under pressure by tightening the nuts in both ends. Use washers to protect the cork so that it will not be deformed. If you have tape on the threaded rod it usually releases from the rod if you have you happened to glue the rings to it, in which case you will have to file off all the tape from the middle hole afterwards. If the threaded rod is sufficiently thick without tape you can insulate it with household plastic wrap. Remove all the plastic carefully from the insert before it is glued onto the blank. Grease, oil and other types of releasing agents are not suitable since they weaken the glue joint to the blank. Allow the glue to cure. Before turning later on, unscrew the nuts and check that the section can be taken off.

Making holes lengthways in a small piece of wood

If the reel seat insert is made from a solid piece of wood you have to drill up a more or less centered hole in it so that you can slip it onto the threaded rod. You can of course do it by eye if the thickness of the wood permits you to drill slightly skew. If you have access to an upright drill, a lathe or an upright stand for a hand drill there is a "crafting trick" here to help you to get the hole in the middle.

Measure up and draw a cross to mark the middle of the piece of wood in both ends. Knock a short nail through a wooden board so that the tip of the nail goes through a few millimeters. Support the wooden board under the stand of the upright drill with a clamp, so that the tip of the drill meets the tip of the nail when you pull it down.

Now make a mark with a nail or an awl exactly in the cross on one end of the piece of wood to be drilled. Place the piece of wood end up on the tip of the nail, so that it comes exactly in the mark in the cross. Hold the piece of wood securely with for example a pair of pliers or a clamp so that it will not rotate, and drill down through it from the one cross to the other. Since the tip of the drill exactly meets the tip of the nail that is on the cross on the underside of the piece of wood, a hole drilled from the upper cross will go through to the lower cross, through the middle of the piece of wood. Run the drill at low speed so that it is easier to hold the section still.

*Making a hole in the length of a thin piece of wood. The middle is marked at both ends. The clamped wooden slab has a pin which exactly meets the tip of the drill. **Top:** The piece of wood is supported with its middle mark on the pin during the drilling (**bottom**).*

Turning

When the glue has cured the insert should be shaped. First release the nuts slightly and check that the section can be removed. If it is glued to the rod you will have the best chance of taking it out in vice now, before the turning has made the material in the tube thin. Tighten the nuts again.

In order to turn the wooden section it must be rounded off and not have any sharp edges. The rounder it is before starting to turn it, the easier it will be. Use a rasp to remove the sharp edges and file it as round as you can, before putting it in the chuck of the drill.

The drill should be horizontal. You can support it in a vice, but there are special bench fittings with screw clamps to fasten it to the edge of a table, and which suit most types of drills. The best results are obtained if you run the drill at top speed. When turning reel seat inserts the raw section is generally so short that there is no risk of it starting to pitch, and therefore there is no need for a support in the outer end of the threaded rod. If the section does want to wobble when it is turning, you can drill a hole in a block of wood and support it on the table with a clamp so that the outer end of the section fits into the hole. This will hold it steady and prevent it from vibrating. The

Wooden and cork sections are turned on a drill mounted in a vice. If the turned section tends to pitch you can support the outer end by placing the threaded rod in a hole in a clamped piece of wood. Hold the rasp so that it cuts with the "away side" of the teeth, and support it against the worktable. If the rasp is held under the turned piece it is easier to see the results.

Switch over to sandpaper in good time. Use thin strips and work carefully – both files and sandpaper will work the cork very quickly.

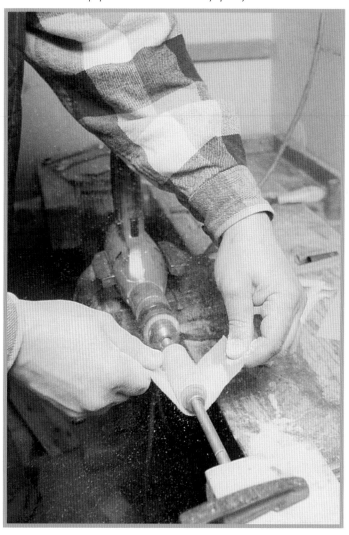

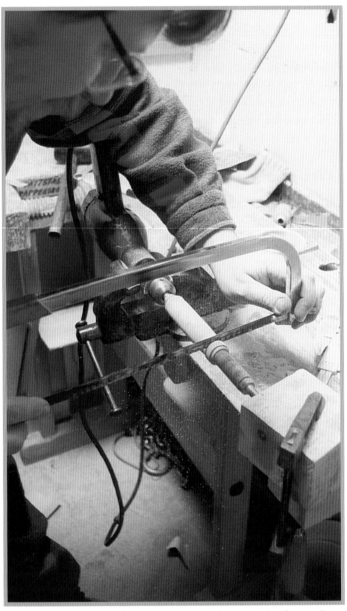

When cutting the turned piece the hacksaw is held against it. When cutting cork you should turn the saw blade "round" to avoid splitting the material.

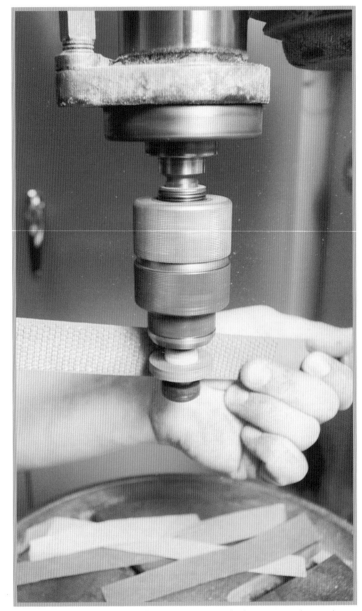

Small wooden parts and wooden rings are turned when mounted on a short bolt. Here in a upright drill, but it works just as well with a drill supported in a clamp.

wood will admittedly become warm and the hole worn after a while, but then you can drill a new hole in the block.

The turning technique can be used for both cork and wood. We are not going to be turning with the help of turning tools in the way we learned in woodwork at school, since thin wooden rings can easily be cracked by a turning tool, and cork will split immediately. The section is "filed" instead by rapid rotation, first roughly with a rasp and then we shape the final

form with narrow strips of sandpaper in increasingly finer grades. The technique works well even without any special support for the file. If the piece is uneven in the beginning, use the table as a support. Hold the rasp with the point resting against the tabletop and press it lightly to the piece so that it only takes the surfaces that "stick out". Do not apply too much pressure until you have got it quite smooth.

To obtain precision in the "rasping" you can support the

end of the file against the table under the rotating section and press it up against the section from underneath. When roughly shaping cork you should even turn the rasp in the "wrong" direction so that the teeth take in the same way as you were pulling the rasp towards you when filing normally. Cork is soft and a rasp can otherwise easily cut off too much material before you can stop yourself.

Go over to sandpaper in good time. Work with narrow strips and check the thickness of the grip frequently. Change over to fine-grained sandpaper and work very carefully – cork is soft and you can easily take off too much in haste. If the section is of wood you can work a bit harder and use a cabinet file or rasp first before going over to sandpaper.

The secret is the rapid rotation, which produces a round result and without irregularities. It is important to get the section completely round before switching over to sandpaper, and if you have succeeded with that it will most often stay round during the rest of the turning with sandpaper, which is because of the rapid rotation. The high speed also gives the cork a fine and attractive surface.

Slide backwards and forwards along the section with the strips of sandpaper to that the turning is uniform all over. You can fix sharp edges in the ends, cuts and ends with a piece of folded sandpaper which is allowed to cut into the cork, or with a hacksaw blade for wood. The hacksaw blade can also have its teeth turned in the "wrong" direction to avoid splitting. Fine sand the surface with increasingly fine-grained sandpaper and polish it finally with a wad of steel wool.

Thin down the ends of the section so that the reel seat thread and the house cap fit. On wooden inserts you can put the house cap on directly without the reel seat piece under, in which case the insert should have the same diameter in the end as the original reel seat. Surfaces to be glued are not fine sanded – the glue adheres better to a rough surface.

Smaller wooden parts such as butts, check rings and effect rings are turned while mounted on a short bolt, where appropriate built up with masking tape. When shaping thin wooden rings you have to work carefully so as to avoid cracking them. Work with the rasp and saw turned in the "wrong" direction so that the teeth are aligned with the direction of rotation – this will make the cutting rate about right. After the turning you can glue a short wooden peg in the hole of the future butt that was rounded in the drill. It is later glued inside the lower end of the blank.

Wood and cork together

Quite often you will want to combine wood and cork. On a grip for example you may want to have effect rings of wood, or make the butt, transitions between grip and reel seat, grip and rod blank (check ring), or other connections between different parts of the grip, out of wood. Other materials such as thin discs of hard plastic, or even metal plate, can also be used to create effects. You make all these sections by means of a hole saw.

When making combinations of wood and cork all the wood must be shaped before it is glued together with the cork. The cork is turned down to the wooden ring, which is well centered.

When putting parts of a somewhat harder material in cork it is important not to turn them together. Cork is so soft and easy to sand that a rasp, file or sandpaper will work on the cork much faster than on most other materials. If you try to turn them together this will only result in the harder materials forming annoying ridges and irregularities. Wooden rings in a cork grip will become raised rings or ridges round the grip, which are not comfortable to hold.

To succeed with effect parts made of harder materials in cork you must always shape these to their finished form

Switch to fine sandpaper in good time and turn down to the cork surface.

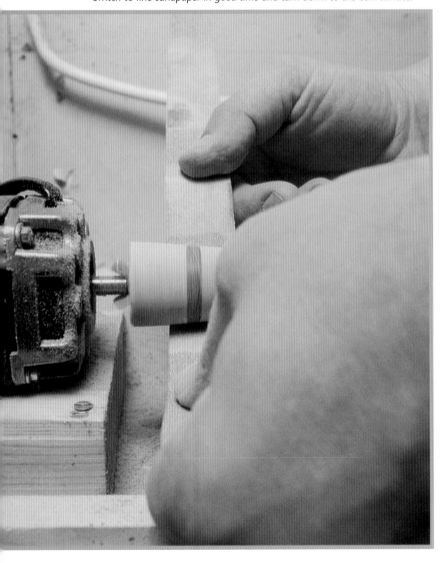

before gluing them in the cork section. The cork is then turned and sanded down to precisely the same surface as the wooden part. When using this method you always have to be careful with the centering of the wooden parts, and to make sure that they rotate absolutely uniformly, otherwise the turning will take the cork down to the surface of the wooden part on one side while there will still be material left on the other, which leads to problems.

Reel seat inserts with a different shape

A rod grip should offer a comfortable and reliable grip, this is one of the basic prerequisites. On spinning rods you grip just over the reel foot and the shape of the grip just there is often not optimal on traditional reel seats. If you want to improve the grip and comfort you can experiment by allowing the reel seat insert to swell out as in a knife handle just over the reel foot. A small "bulge" there fits well into the hand and gives a more comfortable grip.

This type of reel seat insert can be shaped by a combination of the above turning technique and then by shaping the final form by hand. You can start by turning an insert that swells out in all directions to the size you want the "bulge" to have. On the side the reel foot is to be placed you the plane down the insert so that it corresponds with the rest of the reel seat. You can do this with a sanding machine or by pulling the cork on a piece of sandpaper lying flat on a table in the same way as described above. Finally, round off and shape the final finish by hand.

This is a good example of what creativity can achieve, and I return to the reasoning on traditions and innovative thinking – there is no reason for a reel seat to look like a standard reel seat if something else is better. But this is not something I can teach, it is an ability that every one of us must develop for themselves.

Surface treatment

Cork is not surface treated, but wood must be well protected from water and normal varnish is not good enough – it cracks and comes off in the course of time. Treat all wooden parts with epoxy or polyurethane lacquer intended for outdoor use. Allow the wooden parts to lie in a thinned bath of lacquer for an hour or so to absorb it. After curing the pieces are sanded and lacquered several times until all the pores are filled. If you cut or file the parts after the lacquering, you must lacquer them again.

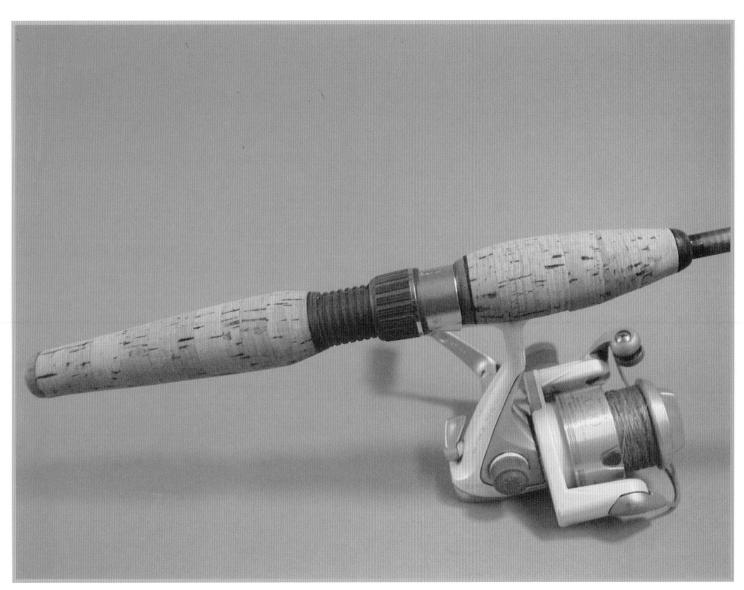

Spinning rod grip shaped to fit comfortably in the hand.

Making the grip

A fishing rod grip should fit well in the hand and suit its user and their casting style. It is therefore important to think through the grip and its function carefully. If for example you have large hands it is possible than many grips will feel too small and slender to hold – this is tiring. It is just as annoying to fish all day with a rod that has a grip that is too thick.

Fly rod grips with a far too strongly tapering shape at the top can lead to the hand slowly but surely moving upwards until you are more or less holding the blank where it connects to the grip. It is therefore important that the upper part of the grip provides a good support and a good hold. On heavier fly rods a somewhat bulged front end is often best, it provides more support for the hand that is handling the rod. On lighter rods a tapering grip gives better control. With a little reflection you can obtain a grip that in similarity with the handle of hand-made knife fits the hand well.

The grip should not be longer than necessary since to a certain extent it dampens the action of the blank. If there is space for the hand to get a comfortable hold then this will be enough. The balance of the rod must also be taken into consideration, and a short grip can result in the rod feeling front heavy. With a longer grip you hold it further up on the rod, and this give a better balance. If the rod still feels front heavy it is possible to weigh it down at the bottom before the butt is glued on.

On two-hand rods the length of the user's arms if of importance. You should be able to utilize the full length of the grip when fishing. Unused length on the grip is unnecessary length, and the action of the blank is only dampened by the cork facing so that it cannot be fully utilized. Some types of rods and certain styles of casting also imply that you change your hold and move the rod from one hand to the other when switching from casting to fishing in. In this case a grip that is too long can cause problems.

Right: Two spinning rod grips shaped to fit well in the hand when fishing with the rod. The metal surfaces are minimized to improve comfort when it is cold.

Far right: The shape of the grip requires careful consideration and planning. Should it be short or long, thick or thin? Swellings and markings where you normally hold it ensure a more secure and comfortable grip.

Types of grips, purposes and effects

The fore grip has almost no function at all on most casting or spinning rods. On a spinning rod you hold it directly over the reel foot both during casting and fishing in. It can happen that you hold it in front of the reel when fishing in with a casting rod, but it is just as common, perhaps even more common, to hold it over the reel, e.g. over the reel head on a level-wind reel. And if you do not move your hand over the reel when playing fish, then the fore grip is not used in any stage of the fishing.

If this is the case you should perhaps think the matter over about whether there should be a fore grip on the rod at all. It would then only be for cosmetic reasons. A fishing rod grip without a fore grip might look strange, but if we have the ambition to free ourselves from traditions and think along new lines even this motivation is lost. Moreover, it is better to

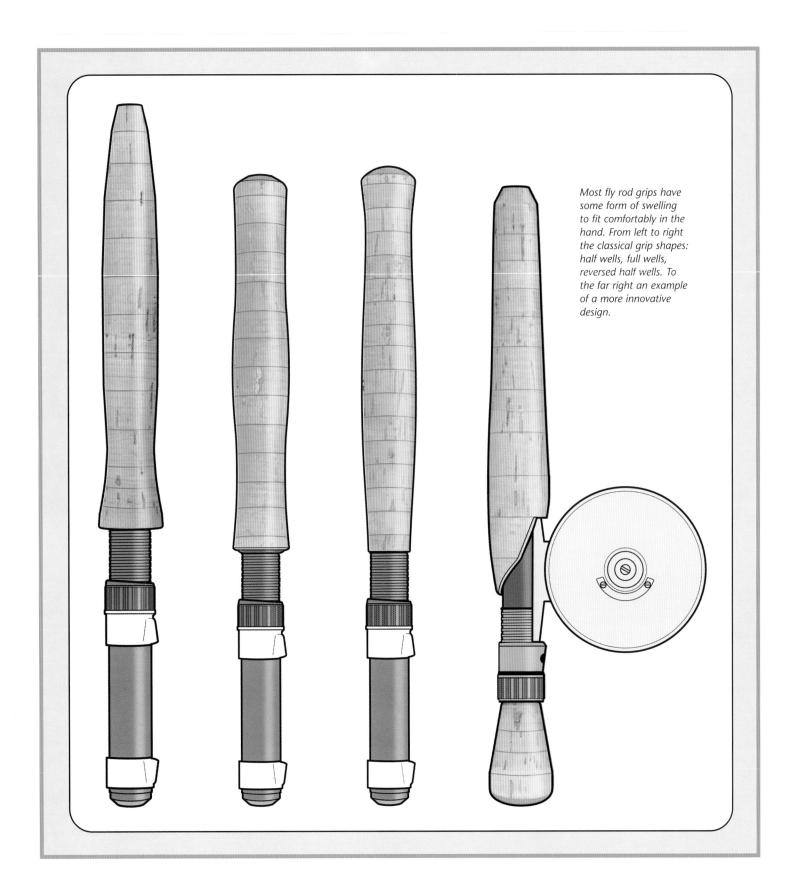

Most fly rod grips have some form of swelling to fit comfortably in the hand. From left to right the classical grip shapes: half wells, full wells, reversed half wells. To the far right an example of a more innovative design.

There are many parallels with knife crafting and the crafting of fishing rod grips, both in terms of shape and materials. Cork inserts help to keep the weight of the grip down.

release the action of the blank than to dampen it with unnecessary cork facing. It might perhaps be a better idea to exclude the fore grip completely, or to reduce it to a connection between the upper end of the reel seat and the blank.

Another part of the grip that is very seldom used in practical fishing is the butt grip's middle section on two-hand spinning and casting rods. When casting you hold it by the reel and at the bottom, and when fishing in you normally clamp the rod grip under your arm in one way or another. If this is the case it might be a good idea to divide the grip up and to leave the blank in the middle of the butt grip bare. For the same reason it is also a good idea to shape the lower part of grip and the grip at the reel with a view to making them fit well in the hand.

With this type of reasoning it almost seems as if we are on our way to drawing the conclusion that a grip is not even needed, but perhaps we should stop ourselves from going so far. What I want to point out is the way of continuously taking the function and role of the grip in practical fishing into consideration when designing your fishing rod grip, without traditional prototypes.

The same applies to other types of rods. On two-hand fly rods the butt grip is shorter and the length varies. There are many people who prefer a very short butt grip with a large knob at the bottom to grip when casting. Perhaps the butt grip would benefit from being reduced to only this knob?

The grips on one-hand fly rods are something of a favorite subject. A good grip fits comfortably in the hand, the hand is in contact with the reel during the cast, the grip provides a good support in its upper end for the thumb or forefinger, whichever style you use, and the mass of the reel is centered in the hand. Moreover, all fly rods, no matter how light they are, benefit from having a butt.

Full wells, half wells and cigar shapes are traditional grip shapes for fly rods. A full well grip swells out both in its upper and lower end, while it has a widening in the middle to fit comfortably in the hand. A half well lacks the upper swelling of the full well, but otherwise is the same. A cigar shaped grip narrows as the name implies at both ends from a thicker middle.

These are shapes that have proved to function well for a long time. The full well grip with its upper swelling functions best for heavier one-hand fly rods since it provides support for the cast when you apply pressure. The narrower upper ends on the half well and cigar grips are best suited for precision casting with lighter rods, without demanding long casts. It is once again important to avoid traditional thinking. On the basis of these types of grips you can create new ones, your own one that better meets the requirements you personally have for a fly rod grip.

When shaping grips and reel seats there is a closely associated craft that can provide a lot of good ideas if you take a look at it, and this is knife crafting. Hand-made knives are of course uncompromisingly made with the precise objective that they should be beautiful and fit comfortably in the hand, something that can give the rod crafter a lot of inspiration.

The shapes of knife grips often function very well on rods.

This also refers to the choice of materials. Knife crafters use in similarity with rod crafters special hardwoods in their grips, but also work with birch bark, leather, horn of various types, silver, tin and other metals, and many other materials. The knife crafter has no need to keep the mass of the grip down, a good knife fits the hand well and has little weight, and so he has more freedom in the choice of materials. But if we select and position our materials in the rod grip with care the result of their weight can instead help to balance the rod. By combining cork with a sufficient number of materials selected from the knife crafter's range of materials we can keep the weight of the grip down,

Balance

A one-hand fly rod should balance somewhere in its upper end or just over it, meaning that it should be evenly balanced just about there. If the rod is too light in the butt it will be

A well-balanced fly rod should, with the reel mounted, balance evenly somewhere in the front part of the grip.

front-heavy, which is tiring to fish with for a full day, regardless of how light the rod is as a whole. If the rod is too heavy in the butt it will be back-heavy and invite wrist casting, which destroys the fly cast. In which case you have to continuously concentrate on your casting style, which is mentally tiring.

For the same reasons a spinning rod should balance approximately at the reel or just over it, and a casting rod at the reel. The balance is achieved with the choice of materials and shape of the grip, by placing the reel sufficiently high up on the rod, and with weights. A grip that is too short on a one-hand spinning or casting rod makes the rod front-heavy – if the reel comes higher up it will balance better. If there are wooden parts in the butt grip they will help to balance up the rod through their mass and weight and if nothing else helps you can glue in balancing weights in the butt on the rod.

Crafting methods

There are two basic methods of making a fishing rod grip. Either you glue cork rings directly on the blank, after which you shape the grip by hand if you have not got a rod lathe, or alternatively you make the grip ready before mounting it on the blank. Both methods have advantages and disadvantages. We are going to concern ourselves with the latter method, above all because a loose grip can easily be shaped by using a standard drill. This produces a better result than shaping the cork by hand, and it is not our intention that we should need advanced machines, such as rod lathes, to achieve a good result.

Good cork is often sold as solid pieces, and sometimes you will also need to change the size of the holes in ready-drilled cork rings. Standard wood drills in a drill running at top speed function well for the purpose of making holes in cork. The top speed makes the holes fine and smooth. Otherwise you can easily make a cork drill from a metal tube of a sufficient size

A long grip shaped directly on the blank in the rod lathe.

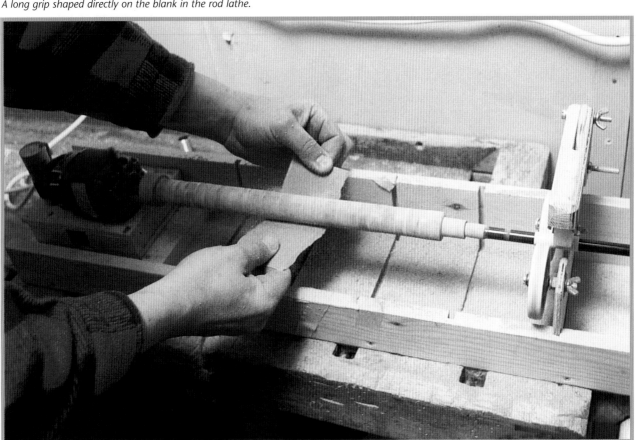

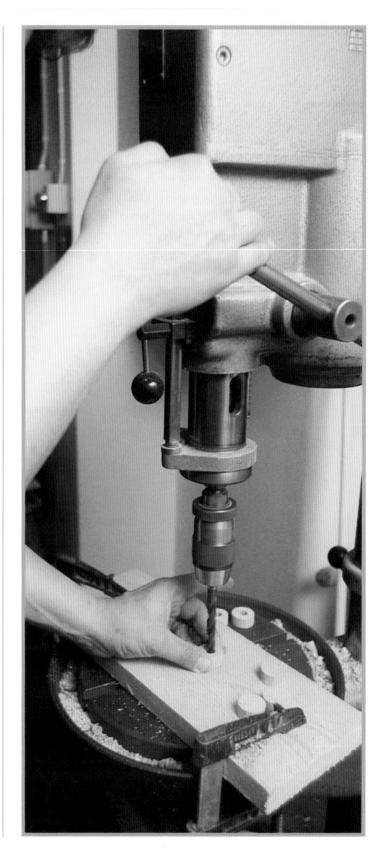

Cork drills can be bought from chemical suppliers, but can also be made from a tube sharpened at one end.

Cork can be drilled with a standard drill, or as shown here with an upright drill. The cork ring is held by hand and the drill runs at top speed. A mark on the wooden slab under the cork ring makes it easier to get the hole in the middle.

and ground sharp in one end. The tube is pressed down in the cork with a rotating movement and cuts out a plug. Ready-made cork drill sets can also be bought from many companies that sell laboratory equipment.

The size of the hole in the cork ring can later be adjusted with a round file, if it should fail to fit on the blank. To make sure that the hole is centered in the cork ring we use the previously described method of turning the ring slightly after each stroke of the file. Check the fit when the file goes round a turn, the ring should preferably sit firmly in position on the blank without sitting too tight. If the holes in the cork rings are too large from the beginning, this is no problem as long as there is not an enormous difference. We fill slightly larger holes with tape and glue so that the grip sits firmly on the blank.

Gluing together a grip section

When you have finished making the holes and the adjustments the cork rings should be glued together to form a grip section. A threaded metal rod functions as a core and clamp. I described how this was done in the section on reel seats.

Cork is best glued with contact glue, this gives a soft and elastic joint and approximately the same sanding characteristics as the cork. Skip a joint here and there if the grip is long, so that the finished grip section is divided up. Sub-sections of a few decimeters are easier to take off after the glue has cured, and when the grip is mounted on the blank it is easier to get the glue to fill out completely under a short grip part than under a long two-hand grip.

Slip all the cork rings on the threaded rod – where appropriate

Cork rings glued together to one unit on a threaded rod built up to the right diameter with masking tape.

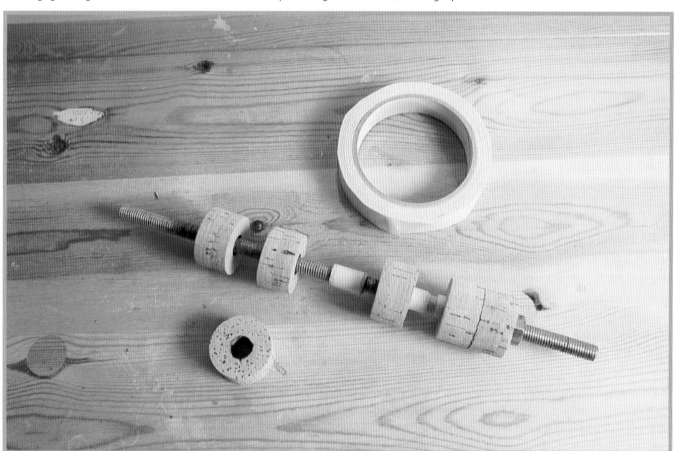

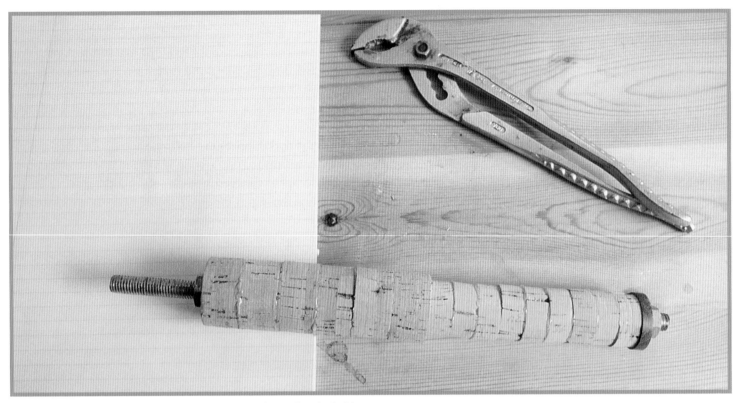

While the glue sets the cork rings are pressed together with nuts from both sides.

built up with masking tape – and press together with the nuts. Effect rings of wood or another hard material must be glued into the grip section together with the cork rings. All such parts should first be turned to their final shape, and preferably lacquered. Cork is softer than wood and it is not possible to turn two materials with such different degrees of hardness together. The holes in the wooden rings should correspond precisely with the cork rings, otherwise they will be difficult to center on the threaded rod. Make sure that the wooden parts in particular are centered, otherwise there will be a problem with the turning!

Turning the grip

When the glue has dried you check that the grip section can be removed from the threaded rod, after which the nuts are tightened again. Just as when you make reel seat inserts, the lathe is a drill supported horizontally on the edge of a table.

A rod grip is sufficiently long for there to be a risk of the threaded rod wobbling during the turning. A wooden block with a hole for the end of the threaded rod is therefore supported on the table with a clamp. Run the drill at top speed and turn

as previously described by means of a file and narrow strips of sandpaper. If a lot of material is to be removed you can use a rasp. Turn the rasp so that you file in the "wrong" direction with the teeth in the direction of rotation. Switch to sandpaper in good time, and observe care. Sharp edges and ends can be fixed with a piece of folded sandpaper or a hacksaw blade. The hacksaw blade should also have the teeth in the "wrong" direction.

If there are wooden rings in the section you carefully cut down the cork flush with their surface, the last bit with very fine sandpaper. The ends of the grip must fit to the ends, which are not glued to the cork yet – check ring, butt or reel seat. Check with sliding calipers. Finish with sandpaper grade 400 over the whole grip. It does not matter if any wooden parts are given a light sanding with this sandpaper, and if the lacquer surface is matt we can lacquer it up again when the rod is ready.

Filling cork

If during the turning the corks proves to contain more holes than expected you can still save the grip by filling the holes. The fillings will be visible to a certain extent but this is better than

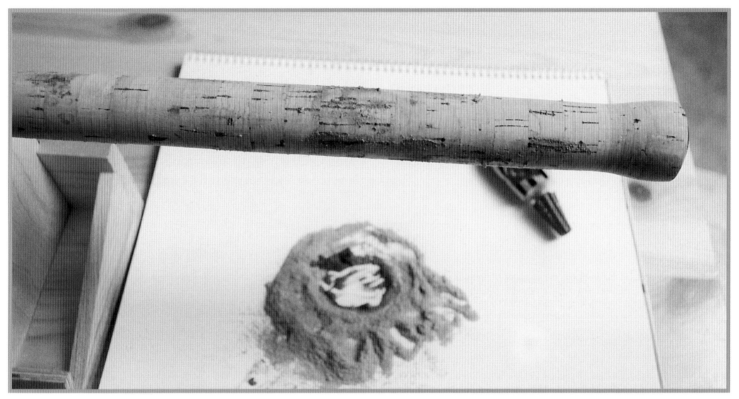

You can fill inferior cork with a filler made from cork dust mixed with standard hobby glue.

leaving them as they are since they will constitute a weakness in the surface of the grip and small pieces could be broken off later. Make a paste of cork powder from the sanding and standard hobby glue. Fill the holes, allow to dry and sand again to make the surface smooth. If necessary repeat the procedure.

The upper part of the grip

There should be a neat transition from the upper end of the grip to the blank. There may often be a small space between the cork in the grip and the blank if the inner hole in the grip cork has been slightly larger than the diameter of the blank. A space like this can be concealed and sealed with a check ring.

You can buy ready-made check rings of various diameters in plastic or rubber, and you can also use a standard rubber O-ring. But it is more attractive and more personal if you make the check ring from cork or wood so that it matches the reel seat insert and trim rings in the grip.

If you are going to make a check ring from cork or wood you must not glue to the upper end of the grip before the grip is mounted. Firstly, the inner holes of the parts may not correspond, the purpose of the check ring being of course to conceal a gap between the grip and blank. Secondly, you sometimes need to fine-adjust the inner hole of the check ring when mounting to make sure it fits precisely, and if it is fitted to the grip there is a risk that you will also have to file the inside of the grip.

On the other hand it is important that its outer shape corresponds with the grip, so that the two parts form one unit when they are glued together. For this reason it is a good idea if the check ring is shaped first, or together with the grip. I have mentioned how you turn thin wooden rings in the chapter on reel seat inserts. As a rule it is possible to arrange tape fillings on the threaded rod so that you can have the check ring in position, pressed against the grip by the nuts, when the grip is turned. This makes it easy to achieve a neat transition between the parts. If this cannot be done you will have to use the sliding calipers and check regularly and carefully when the parts are shaped.

The butt

The lower end of the grip should also be finished off with a butt cap or rod butt. You can also buy these ready-made, usually in rubber or plastic, but once again cork and wood will function here too. One way of making a butt is to turn a cork ring or a wooden ring – made with a hole saw – to a suitable shape by the same method used for trim rings and check rings. When the butt is ready you glue a peg in its inner hole, and when the grip is ready you glue the peg into the lower hole on the blank so that grip sits firmly in place.

If the butt is made of wood you can make the peg from a peg of the same species of wood, rounded off in a drill until it fits the wooden ring. Plastic, metal and other durable materials can also be used. If you do not want the end of the peg to be visible in the cork or wood, you glue it in such a way that it does not go completely through the outside of the butt. The end of the peg is then covered by gluing a piece of cork or wood in the hole on the outside of the butt, and then sanding it down so that the surface becomes smooth.

Butts for fly rods. At the front three butt plates of the type supplied with most fly rod reel seats. You can also fit your rod with a fighting butt (over these). From the left a hand-made cork butt to glue directly on the blank, a purchased detachable butt (the sleeve is glued into the reel seat at the bottom) and a hand-made variety. To the right a butt of reindeer horn with attendant house cap, and a butt of masur birch, reindeer horn and tin.

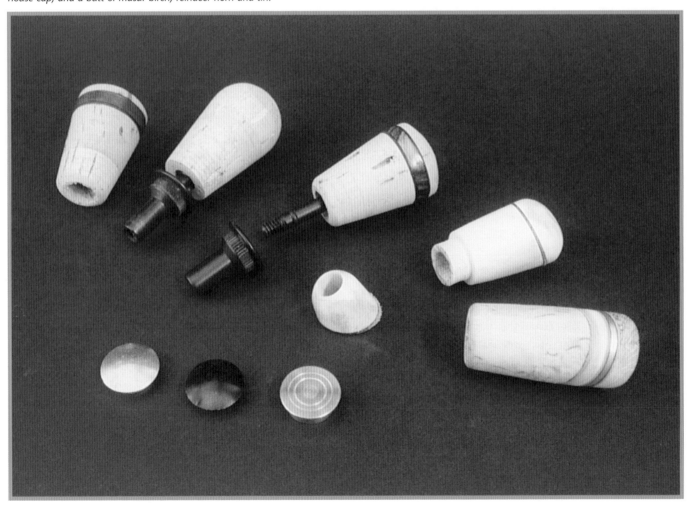

Mounting the grip and reel seat

During the mounting procedure all the grip parts are pushed down over the blank from the top. If their inner holes are too large you build up the blank with masking tape, and if the holes are too small you file them up with a round file. If you work in the same way described earlier when filing, then the holes will remain centered in the grip.

Roughen up the inner surface of the reel seat and the surface on the blank where the grip is to sit with rough sandpaper. This instruction may produce a surprised reaction – can you really scratch the blank – will it not weaken it! But it is quite correct, we are going to produce scratches and marks in the bright lacquer surface to achieve a completely strong glue joint between the grip and blank. Epoxy functions a little differently than standard glues based on solvents.

If for example you are gluing with normal joiner's glue it is important that the glue surfaces are uniform and smooth and lie as close to each other as possible. This because the glue penetrates into the material a little, and because it shrinks when the solvent disappears. Epoxy is the best glue for rod crafting purposes precisely because it does not function through evaporation of a solvent and does not shrink when it cures. Neither does it penetrate into the material, especially not into the metal of the reel seat or the epoxy cured carbon fibers of the blank. On the other hand it grips and adheres very well to a naked surface, and even better the rougher the surface is.

By roughening up the surface of the blank we create irregularities that the epoxy can fill out and grip, and the glued joint therefore becomes far much stronger. It is not our intention to go so deep that we go through the lacquer down into the carbon fiber material, just scratch the lacquered surface of the blank a little with a piece of rough sandpaper! This does not necessarily need to be done, and definitely should not be done on a matt blank. A matt surface already has small microscopic irregularities for the glue to adhere to, and since it is matt it is much more difficult to determine how deep you can go and how thick the layer of lacquer is.

If the inner hole of the grip or the reel seat is larger than the diameter of the blank you have to build it up with tape in the same way as we did on the threaded rod. But we must absolutely not build up a continuous tape cylinder that covers the whole blank surface under the grip. The grip and reel seat should be glued to the blank, not to a layer of tape, in which

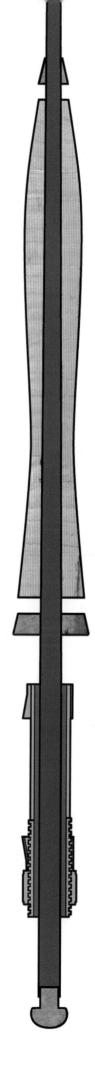

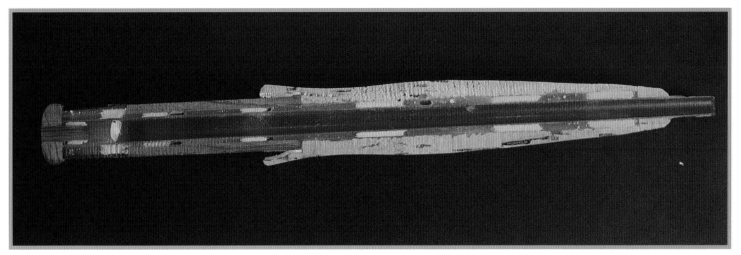

Cross section of a grip on the blank. The reels of tape and the glue that fills out the intervening spaces can be clearly seen.

Top left: The bright surface of a blank is roughed up with sandpaper before the grip is glued on.

Bottom left: The reel seat with inserts of wooden and cork rings for the fore grip is ready to be mounted on the blank. Where the diameter of the blank is too small it is built up with well-spaced reels of tape.

case only the adhesive power of the tape would hold the grip in place. We want instead to cover as little as possible of the blank with tape under the grip, so that the glue can fill out and grip the surface of the blank all over between the tape.

Wrap hard, narrow reels of tape as bushings at regular intervals under the whole grip, thinly enough so that no more than half of the blank surface is covered with tape, preferably less. When you apply the glue it should fill all the spaces between the reels of tape. When the glue has cured it will form hard epoxy bushings between the reels of tape, and this is where the strength of the glue joint is.

Masking tape will not stick to a surface that is moist with epoxy, which means that you will have a problem if in the middle of the gluing you realize that there is a reel of tape missing somewhere. The only solution is to wash the blank clean, leave any parts in place to cure, and then start from the beginning with the remaining parts. For this reason think carefully through the mounting procedure and test with all parts in position before you begin to glue. If the grip is a long one and contains a large number of parts it can be better to divide the work up into stages and allow the glue to hard in-between.

Think also carefully through which order the parts are to be put on the blank. All the parts are slipped on the blank from the top, and we start the work of mounting them with the bottom part and then work up the grip in sequence. If a part, e.g. the reel seat, has a larger inner diameter than the grip parts that are to be placed below it, you will need thicker tape bushings under it than under the parts that are placed further down on the blank. In this case they cannot be slipped past the position of the reel seat and it will be necessary to do the mounting in stages. Mount the grip from the bottom and up as far as possible in one go, allow the glue to dry, put on new tape bushings for the thicker part above the other positioned parts, and continue the work.

If the reel seat has several different parts, e.g. if it is divided with a reel seal insert in the middle, the mounting will be easier if you glue on the thread and house cap so that you have a complete reel seat before you put it on the blank.

Gluing on the grip

We therefore begin mounting from the bottom, with the exception that we leave the butt until last so that the lower end of the blank remains open. If the rod needs to be balanced with weights these should be glued in before the butt is glued in position, and we will not know if this is necessary before the rod guides are fitted. We may also need to fine sand the grip after the gluing and if the butt end is open you can sometimes set it rotation, which simplifies the sanding.

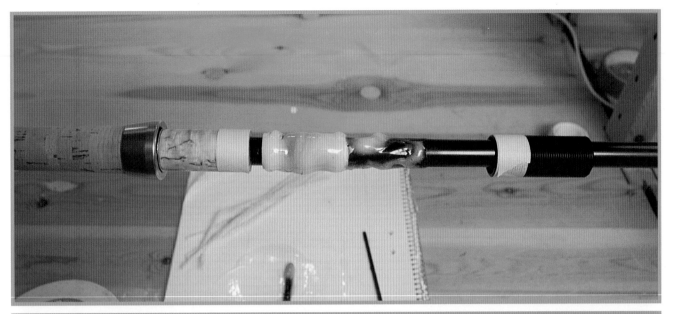

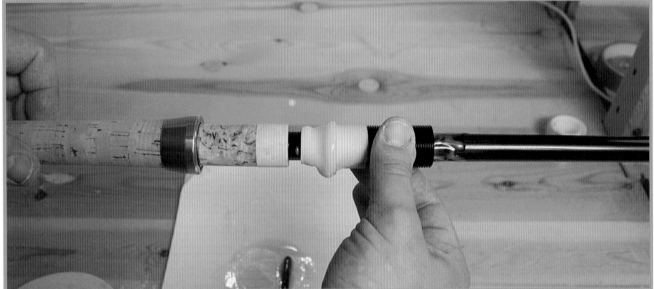

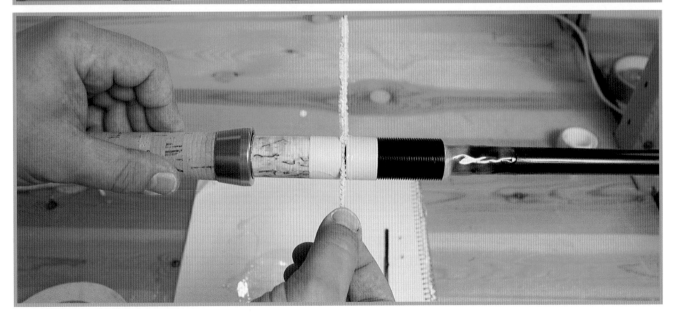

All the parts, both the grip and reel seat, are mounted in the same way. Mix the two components for the epoxy – base and hardener – carefully according to the manufacturer's instructions. To protect the surface of the grip from stains we place masking tape round the ends on the grip part that is to be mounted. Place the blank horizontal on a pair of supports of the same type used during the gluing. A newspaper underneath protects the worktable from dripping glue. Smear a thick layer of glue on the blank from the section to be glued, i.e. the place where the grip you are fitting is to sit, and a good bit upwards. Fill all the spaces between the tape reels completely with glue. There should also be ample glue at least a few decimeters over the final destination for the grip part we are fitting.

The idea of applying glue so far up is that all the spaces under the grip and reel seat should be filled with glue! When the grip part is moved down over the blank it will push a bank of glue in front of it, and from this bank glue will flow in-between the blank and grip. By turning the parts all the time in relation to each other you spread the glue evenly under the grip. The glue is pressed forward over the blank in front of the grip part while you move it down, and each time you pass over the tape bushings described above the glue will "sink" down in the space and completely fill the area between the grip and blank.

This should not be done too quickly. Rotate the parts, the grip and blank, while you are working so that the glue does not drip off the blank. Stop at the end of each tape filling so that the bank of glue can sink down and fill the depression between them completely. Stop a little just before the grip part reaches its final destination and remove the bank of glue. First let most of the surplus run off onto the newspaper, it is

Top: House cap and wooden insert in position. The blank is coated with glue, thickly between the reels of tape and a bit upwards. The end of the thread section is protected with masking tape before fitting.

Center: The threaded section is put in place and pushes up a bank of glue in front of it. The glue must fill the space between the threaded part and the blank.

Bottom: Stop just before the parts are put together, let surplus glue run off, and remove the last of it with a pipe cleaner. Push together the parts and wash with denatured spirit.

reused when the next part is fitted, and then use a pipe cleaner to remove the rest. When there is only a thin coating left press the parts together. Denatured spirits on a wad of paper or pipe cleaner will dissolve any glue stains. Make sure at the same time that the lower end of the blank is not glued.

Now place new glue on the blank and follow on section by section as far as can be done in one sweep. Remove the bank of glue each time just before the grip parts slide together, but leave a little glue so that the joint will be tight. Clean with spirits, but allow all the masking tape to remain for the time being. When everything is ready wash the blank and grip thoroughly all over with spirits. The masking tapes are now removed and you clean it again if necessary. Carefully check the position of the reel seat in relation to the spine marks. Check also that the house cap has not been filled with glue, or that the lock nuts risks being glued. A pipe cleaner with denatured spirits makes cleaning in the house cap and between the thread simple. Finally put the rod under pressure and allow it to cure.

The glue joints can be put under pressure in many different ways. A description is given in the chapter on tools how you can make a simple grip clamp, and one of these is naturally best. Otherwise you can twine with string or use weights to press together two plates at each end of the grip. Make sure that residual glue on the blank does not adhere to the plates. Pressing is often not necessary if the parts fit "tightly" on the blank.

The check ring is glued in place when the glue has cured, and should have in inner diameter that exactly corresponds with the blank. The pressing will often have pressed the grip together slightly more than anticipated, and since the blank is tapered the check ring will then have come on a slightly thicker part of the blank than it was made for. The difference will only be slight. Adjust with a round file according to the description above until it fits, and then glue with epoxy.

On long rod grips that are mounted in sections there may be traces or smears of glue at the joints. Such smears can easily be removed by sanding with fine-grained sandpaper. The best results will be obtained if you can rotate the grip, which is possible if you have a rod lathe with roll support. Do not attempt to place the blank in the wrapping rack and run with the drill, since the frictional heat that develops when it runs against the felt protection on the wrapping rack can damage it.

Positioning the guides

The positioning of the guides influences the precision, balance and cast length in several different ways. We have already discussed the function of the spine and how it can be utilized. We have also gone through how the mass of the guides has an effect on the casting and playing characteristics, and how the wraps that hold the guides can change the action of the rod. We will now discuss how the positioning of the guides along the length of the blank distributes the strains and stresses on the rod.

Most rod building kits and rod blanks are delivered with a guide spacing table. If you follow this then everything is easy, both the number of guides and their positioning can be read from the table. But you will loose an important dimension in your rod crafting hobby if you place the guides according to a table. First of all and quite obviously, if you get used to working from a guide spacing table you will become helpless when one is not available – which is bound to happen sooner or later. Less obvious, but even more important is that the guide spacing table does not always give the best possible positioning of the guides for the rod.

The table represents a compromise, an average based on a number of random samples from the manufacturing series, but then each blank is individual. If you are lucky the difference between the blank you are building and the "average blank" the table is based on will be rather marginal, but it could just as easily be rather significant. Placing the guides in a way that takes into consideration the characteristics of the blank – so that you achieve maximum performance – is central to successful rod crafting.

The purpose of the guides is not only to lead the line from the reel up to the tip of the rod, if this had been the case it would in many cases be enough with a top ring. The guides also distribute the stain evenly along the rod when you are casting or playing fish with it. It is only by placing the guides in an optimal way that you can fully utilize the strength of the blank.

The guides must be set out along the length of the rod so that all parts of the blank do their part of the work, and no part of it is overloaded. Moreover, you must also take into consideration where the mass of the guides ends up so that the inherent mass of the rod does not slow down the action too much, and finally you must take into consideration how the line behaves when it passes through the guides, since the braking effect of the guides on the line influences the casting length.

In casting and spinning rods it is first and foremost a question of the side movements in the line that have to be dampened when it passes through the rod guides, while on fly rods it is more about dampening and distributing the directional changes that the relatively stiff and heavy line is exposed to when is passes from the "double pull hand" up through the guides, or when it is shot from the ground, a line basket or the water.

The number of guides

Too few guides on a rod makes it difficult or impossible to find a functioning guide positioning. The rod is exposed to unnecessary strain and this is distributed so unevenly that large spot loads can occur. The blank cannot handle casting to its full potential, and there can be a risk of breaking the rod. Having too many guides results in an unnecessarily large mass, and brakes the action of the rod as we have discussed earlier.

In other words it is a question of striking a balance, and providing definitive rules for the number of guides on a rod is risky – each blank is individual. The following is therefore to be considered as guidelines and individual rods may require one or more guides or less. If you are unsure it is almost always best to go for more rather than less. Bear in mind that you can also change to a lighter type of guide if there are too many. The risk of having the wrong number of guides is in the end almost negligible, and before we are finished it will become quite clear whether we chose the right number of guides from the beginning.

Fly rods normally require one guide per foot of rod length, possibly one guide less on two-hand rods. On spinning rods you deduct two feet from the length of the rod and then calculate one guide per foot. You do the same on casting rods but only deduct one foot from the length of the rod. Some fly rods are improved with one guide more than the norm, assuming that the blank can withstand this. A 9 foot spinning rod would in other words be able to manage with 7 guides, while an equally long casting rod should almost always have 8. A fly rod of the same length would need 9-10 guides. Short rods of all types may need one extra guide over what the norm specifies.

Position the guides temporarily

First glue the top ring correctly in relation to the previously made spine marking. Use 5-minute epoxy or hot-set adhesive since the top ring is the guide that is most exposed and if you knock the rod somewhere it easily happens that the ceramic in it cracks. If the top ring ever needs to be replaced all you have to do is warm the metal sleeve slightly with the flame from a spirit lamp to release the glue joint. All the rest of the gluing on the rod should be done with slow-curing epoxy, but not this one.

When the top ring is mounted all the other guides are set out provisionally. The guides are taped onto the rod so that they can easily be moved, since after this stage there is a careful, step by step test of the positioning of the guides.

The position of the butt guide (closest to the reel, in other words the line guide on a fly rod) is governed by the distance from the reel. Start by placing it 40-70 centimeters from the reel on a casting rod, depending on the length of the rod. On a spinning rod the butt guide should be placed about one third of the distance between the reel foot and tip of the rod. On one-hand fly rods it should sit 70-85 centimeters from the reel, slightly further up on two-hand fly rods.

Guide 1 (this is the one that sits closest to the top ring, we always number the guides from top to bottom) must not sit too far from the top ring! It supports the thin top section and provides protection from tip fracturing. It should sit 10-15 centimeters from the top ring, depending on the length of the rod, and not over 13 centimeters in a one-hand rod.

The other guides can be set out more or less with your naked eye in this first stage. You can start by positioning the guides quite simply by measuring the distance from the butt guide to guide 1 and dividing it up so that the intervals between the guides are the same. In the end all the guides will sit in their correct positions when the guide positioning procedure is finished! But if you do this the distance between the guides in the top part of the blank will be unnecessarily large, and since you have to test cast with the rod to find the correct guide positions this can lead to excessive spot loads and risk breaking the rod as a result.

The relative distance between the guides should of course successively be reduced the closer you come to the top. The blank is softest at the top and consequently bends most there, and where the curvature of the blank is most pronounced the guides should sit most closely together. A better way of starting is to set out the guides by eye with a relative distance between them that successively reduces up towards the tip. You can also follow the guide positioning on another equally long rod of the same type. In this way there is no risk of the rod breaking during the test casting, even if the positioning is still not quite correct.

The taped guides will need to be moved on the blank a number of times before the positioning is ready. There will be quite a lot of tape that needs to taken off and put on, which is a sticky and fiddling job that can be rather tiresome. If you want to make it easier for yourself there are a few alternative methods of temporarily fixing the guides.

Latex hose of the type that surgeons and other medical people use for drains and the other unmentionable things that are part of their trade is perfect for this purpose. Slip on short pieces on the blank before the top ring is fixed on, and use these to hold the guides. Repositioning is now done in a flash, you just roll off the latex hose from the guide foot, move the guide, and roll on the hose again. When the guides are to be wrapped tight you cut off the hose stubs and throw them away.

If you cannot get hold of this type of hose you can use standard O-rings in the same way. An O-ring will not hold the guide feet equally secure, so a couple of them might be needed for each guide foot and the largest guides may need to be secured with tape during test casting. They will also have to be cheap O-rings, since you have to cut them off when they are no longer needed.

Testing the final positioning of the guides

Note than none of the following can be done before the female ferrule is properly glued and coated with a few coats of color preserver.

We start by determining the final position of the butt guide, and we do this by test casting with the rod. Look for a grass lawn, football field or the like where there is sufficient space for you to cast at full force and without having to worry about the direction and distance, or anything else that might be in the way. In this stage you have to be able to concentrate completely on how the rod behaves and you will mainly need to keep an eye on this, and not where the casting weight lands.

Work like this with a spinning rod. Cast with it repeatedly and carefully study how the line behaves in the area between the reel and the butt guide. Stand so that the light comes right. You will see it most clearly if it is reflected off the line and the background is dark. The line leaves the edge of the reel spool in a rather wide spiral, which is constricted when it goes through the butt guide. If the constriction is too hard the line will be braked, which means that the guide is placed too close to the reel and must be moved further up the rod. Move it slightly and cast again. Continue doing this until the line spiral narrows off by itself and glides into the butt guide more or less unaffected.

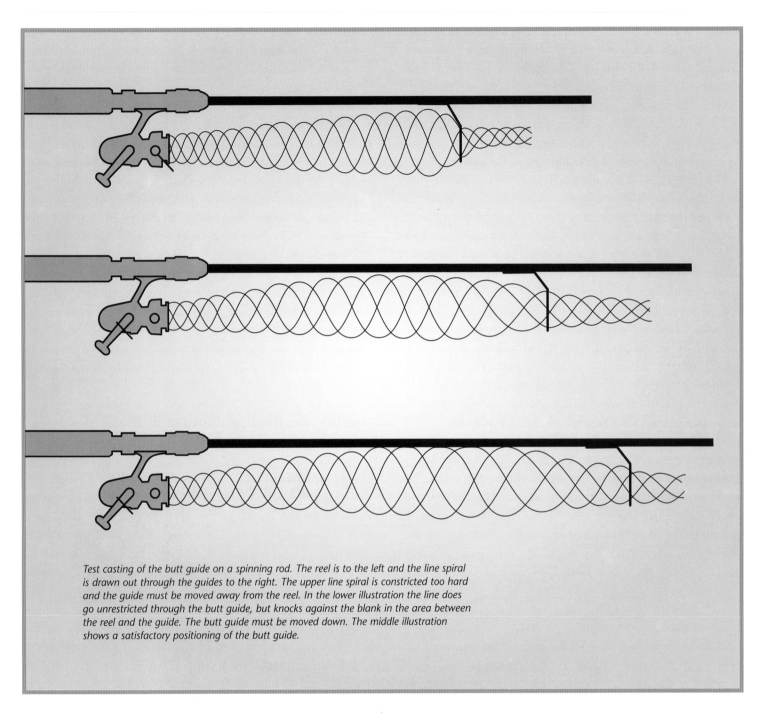

Test casting of the butt guide on a spinning rod. The reel is to the left and the line spiral is drawn out through the guides to the right. The upper line spiral is constricted too hard and the guide must be moved away from the reel. In the lower illustration the line does go unrestricted through the butt guide, but knocks against the blank in the area between the reel and the guide. The butt guide must be moved down. The middle illustration shows a satisfactory positioning of the butt guide.

If the butt guide comes too far away from the reel during this procedure the line spiral will start instead to shake out and whip against the blank in the area between reel and butt guide. This will brake the line even more if this is possible than the above mentioned constriction, and therefore the butt guide must be moved closer to the reel.

In other words it is a question of finding a functioning com-promise between two extremes. If you cannot find a position for the butt guide that satisfied both these requirements you will have to change the butt guide. A guide with a higher keeper reduces the line's contact with the blank. If this does not work, try with a larger guide, which can sit closer to the reel without the constriction effects. Avoid moving the butt guide too far up on the rod, since this can mean that the blank receives too little support in the area closest to the grip. It will then not be utilized effectively when casting and could break when exposed to strain. Try as far as possible to keep the butt guide on a spinning rod close to the mentioned one third of the distance.

Note also the casting length during your experiment. It will not be maximized since the other guides are probably far from correctly positioned, but if it increases while you are working this is an indication that the guide is going in the right direction. If the cast becomes shorter you try moving the guide in the other direction instead.

Casting rods

The problem is almost the same on casting rods. The cross-wise arrangement of the line on the reel means that it leaves the reel with a sideways movement – it swings backwards and forwards sideways. In the other positions it is constricted by the butt guide and braked. In other words the contact between the line and butt guide should be minimized.

Start with a static test. Put the reel on the rod, pull the line through all the guides and tie it to a fixed object. Release the line and move back about ten meters, tighten up with the rod pointing in the direction of the line and then reel in while walking slowly towards the fixed point. If there is so much contact between the line and guide when the line guide is in the outer position that an angle is formed in the line where it passes through the butt guide then you should move the guide up the rod. If there is space left in the outer positions you can move the guide downwards, but you do not need to do this if it is not an extremely long way from the reel.

Try casting it after this in the same way as the spinning rod. If the oscillation of the line in the butt guide is constricted, move the guide up. If the instead the line is braked against the blank between the reel and butt guide, move the line down. Make sure that it does not come too far up on the rod. It is possible to have much larger guides on a casting rod than the ones you can see on factory-made rods. Keep checking the casting length and move the guide slightly backwards and forwards until you are sure you have found the maximum length.

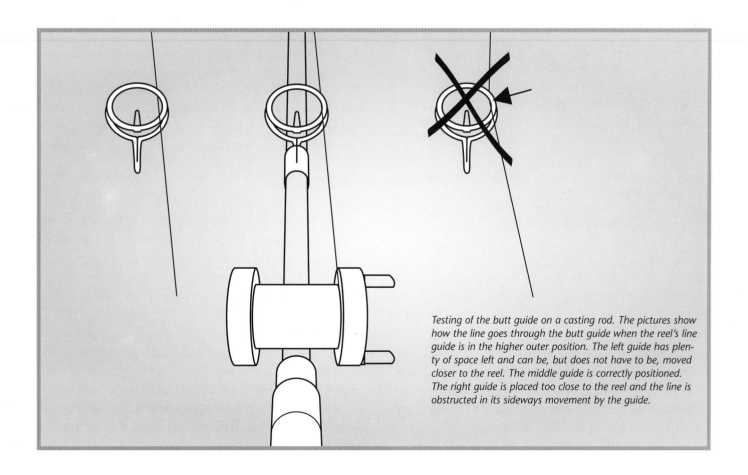

Testing of the butt guide on a casting rod. The pictures show how the line goes through the butt guide when the reel's line guide is in the higher outer position. The left guide has plenty of space left and can be, but does not have to be, moved closer to the reel. The middle guide is correctly positioned. The right guide is placed too close to the reel and the line is obstructed in its sideways movement by the guide.

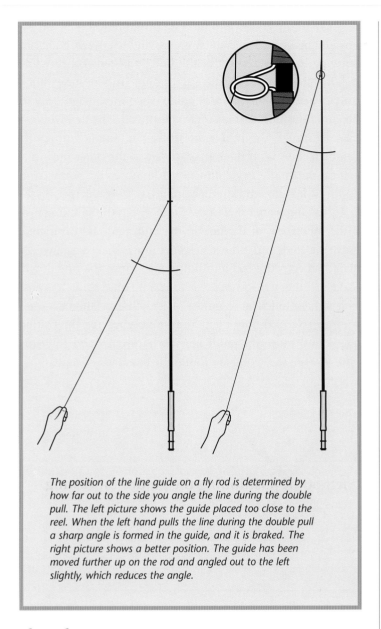

The position of the line guide on a fly rod is determined by how far out to the side you angle the line during the double pull. The left picture shows the guide placed too close to the reel. When the left hand pulls the line during the double pull a sharp angle is formed in the guide, and it is braked. The right picture shows a better position. The guide has been moved further up on the rod and angled out to the left slightly, which reduces the angle.

Fly rods

The mechanics of casting with fly rods is slightly different. The line is shot from the hand, the ground or the water etc. without an actual side movement, although on the other hand it is thicker and stiffer, and comes into the line guide at an angle, somewhat from the side. It is mainly braked by large angles in the line trajectory and by contact with the blank, and it is important that the line is not braked against the blank in the backward cast if you are going to be able to complete an effective double pull.

Test cast and note the angle of the line at the line guide. It

should be as small as possible and the line should not have any contact with blank. The angle in the line at the line guide is caused when the hand performing the double pull is not held directly under the rod. Everyone has their own personal way of doing things, and your own casting style will determine the size of the angle. The angle is reduced if you move the line guide up, but at the same time there is a greater risk that it will be drawn to the blank somewhere between the grip and the line guide, especially in the backward cast.

If you turn the line guide slightly away from the center line of the rod, towards the side the line comes from during a double pull when you shoot the line, you can reduce the line angle without needing to move the guide. A higher guide holds the line further away from the blank and therefore permits a greater distance from the reel. Turning the line guide to the side will have a greater effect on the line angle if the line guide has a higher keeper. Avoid moving the line guide too far up, and keep a check on the casting length.

When the position of the butt guide seems to function, continue casting for a while. Get the feel of the rod, study the behavior of the line at the line guide and in the area between the reel and the line guide, and try to achieve the best casting length possible. It will not be the absolute best because the other guides are not correctly positioned, but try to come as far as you can with the present positioning of the guides. Mark the position of the butt guide and experiment with slight deviations up and down until you find the position that allows you to cast the furthest and shoot the most line.

Other guides

The positioning of the other guides is determined by the bending curve of the blank. The load on the blank is greatest at the mid point between two guides, and reduces to a minimum just at the guide and then increases again to the next mid point between the next pair of guides. If the rod is to be loaded evenly the relative distance between the guides must be adjusted to the capacity of the blank to withstand loading. Fewer guides are needed where the blank is strongest, and most are needed where it is weakest. Consequently, where the rod bends only slightly when loaded the guides can be spaced further apart, and where it bends a lot they should sit closer together.

If you have succeeded in placing all the guides in a way that corresponds to the strength of the blank throughout then the stress will evenly distributed along the rod, and the blank can

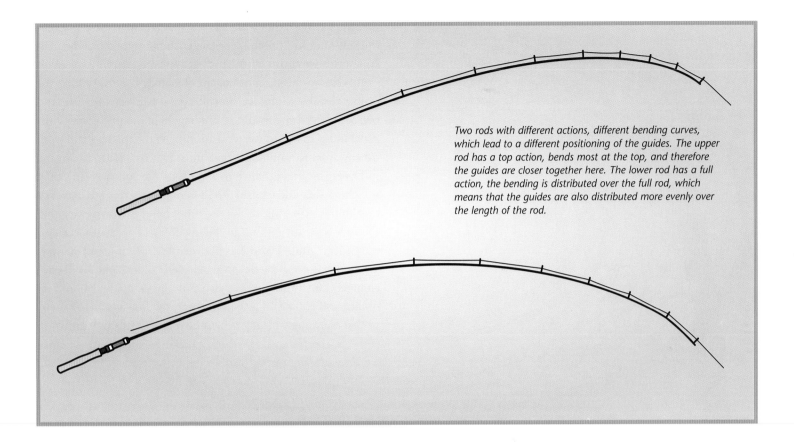

Two rods with different actions, different bending curves, which lead to a different positioning of the guides. The upper rod has a top action, bends most at the top, and therefore the guides are closer together here. The lower rod has a full action, the bending is distributed over the full rod, which means that the guides are also distributed more evenly over the length of the rod.

be fully utilized during the cast. If the guides are spaced further apart in relation to the bending curve of the rod at one place more than at another, then this area will be exposed to spot loads more than the rest of the blank. This will lead to an inferior casting capacity – a chain is only as strong as its weakest link – and the risk of the rod breaking.

When the rod is bent the line goes in a straight line from one guide to the next, forms a slight angle just where it lies against the inside of the guide, and then goes in another straight line to the next guide. During the process of positioning the guides we will try to make these angles all the same. The distance between the line and the blank is greatest at the mid point between two guides if the rod is bent with the guides on the underside, or least if they are placed on topside of the bending curve. We will also try to make these maximum (or minimum) distances between each pair of guides also the same, with the exception of the distance provided by the different heights of the guides. The strain will be evenly divided along the blank if these two conditions are met.

Method of positioning the guides on casting and spinning rods

On rods where the guides have a certain height it is possible to utilize this when testing out the positions of the guides. Put a reel on the rod and fix it in some way so that the tip points upwards at an angle of approximately 45 degrees. I use a plastic tube fixed to a stable object by means of tape or string. I then wrap a piece of cloth round the rod grip to protect the cork, and set it down in the tube so that the reel comes on the topside of the rod.

Pull the line through the guides and anchor the end of the line to the leg of chair, or the like, some distance from the tip of the rod. The line should be able to be stretched up so that the rod forms quite a sharp arc, more or less like when playing a fish. The line is now held up from the curved blank by the guides and comes closest to it at the mid points between the guides.

At certain points the distance between the guides is so great that they cannot keep the line off the rod where it is bent. The line lies flat against the blank and creates a "flat point". This means that the guides are spaced too far apart here because the line should not be in contact with the blank anywhere, in spite of the bending of the rod.

It is now a question of placing the guides so that all the flat points disappear and so that the gaps between the line and blank are the same at all the points where the line comes closest to the blank. Start the repositioning at the top ring and work downwards. Note that guide 1 must not be moved down the rod because if its distance to the tip of the rod is greater than the previously mentioned 10-13 centimeters there is a risk of breaking the tip. Guide 2 on the other hand can be move either up or down until the line and blank are held apart just as much as between guide 1 and 2 as between the top ring and guide 1. When this is done the distance between guide 2 and 3 will have changed, or in other words you now move guide 3 until you obtain and equally large gap between the line and blank there.

You continue working down the blank in this way until you come to the butt guide, which cannot be moved either since we have already put a lot of effort into deciding its position.

Guide positioning on casting and spinning rods. On the upper rod the guides are placed too far apart and a flat point is formed at the arrow (F). To remove this the guides must be moved together. The lower picture shows a better positioning of the guides. The line angle in the guide (red marking at the bottom) should be the same size at all the guides.

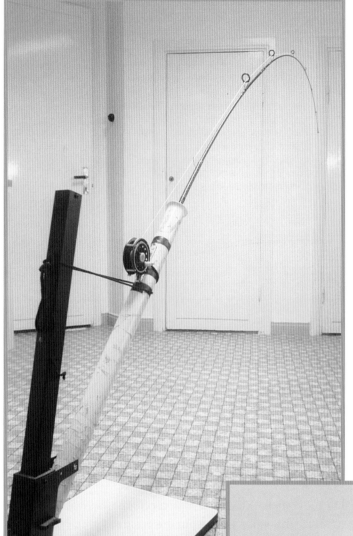

Above: *Home-made device for positioning rod guides. The frame comes from an old photo enlarger, the tube is a piece of a carry case for rod blanks. The fly reel is permanently mounted on the tube and the fly line can be more clearly seen than a nylon line. The rod (in this case a spinning rod) is held in place by piece of cloth wrapped round the grip, and then pushed down in the tube.*

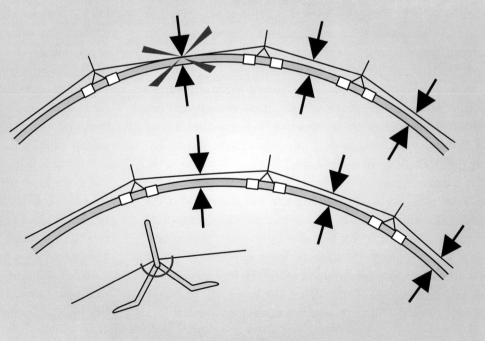

If there is a flat point between the lowest guide and the butt guide then we have too few guides. If this is the case we increase the set of guides by one guide of the smallest size, which we place at the top below guide 1, after which we work our way down the rod again.

The bending curve of the blank changes when the guides are moved, since the load on it is redistributed. When you have found a first uniform distribution it is time to go back and check everything from the beginning again. If necessary go over the positioning of all the guides from the top ring and downwards several times. When all flat points have been eliminated and the gap between the line and blank is the same at each mid point between the pairs of guides, then you are ready. The angles formed by the line when it passes through the guides are now basically the same all over, and the strain when the rod is bent is evenly distributed.

Pay attention to the area between the reel and the butt guide. If the curvature of the blank there seems unproportionally sharp, or if there is a flat point there, then the butt guide is too high up. If so use a larger butt guide and repeat the entire procedure from the beginning, including test casting and all the rest, to bring the butt guide closer to the reel.

Fly rods

Fly rod guides, in particular snake guides, are in general too low to be able to utilize their height in the way described above. Tension up the rod with the guides in the normal position instead, on the underside of the blank, and carefully study the line angles in the guides and the distance between the line and blank where is it greatest, at the mid point between the guides. The line should "follow the rod" smoothly and tightly, without sharp jerks in the line trajectory or irregularities in the distance between the blank and line along the rod. The angles in the line where it passes the guides should be the same. It may be difficult to distinguish the critical points in the beginning, but you can gradually train your eye to gauge a reliable measure.

The positioning of the guides is now ready and it is time to go out and test cast again. It will now be an advantage if you "got a good feel" for the rod during the first test casting. It should now behave as normal, and should definitely cast further then before, and this is when you receive confirmation that the guides are positioned correctly. If the rod feels too pliant or seems to whip, if it does not cast as well you had expected, or if you get the feeling that there is a "hinge" in it somewhere, you should check the positioning of the guides once again, but if you have been careful during the whole procedure this should not be necessary. When you are finally satisfied, measure up and note all the positions of the guides because it is now time to remove them again so that the blank and guides can be prepared for the wrapping work.

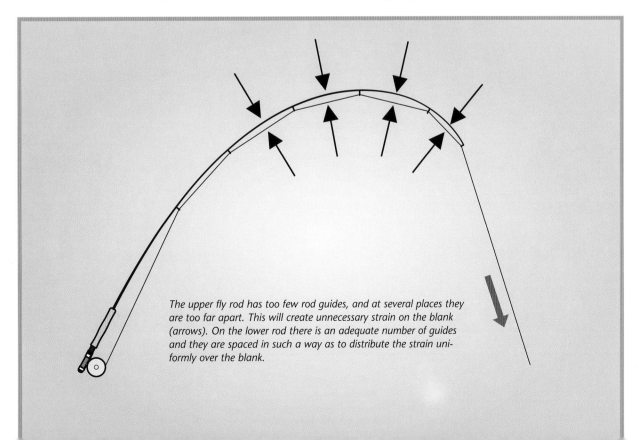

The upper fly rod has too few rod guides, and at several places they are too far apart. This will create unnecessary strain on the blank (arrows). On the lower rod there is an adequate number of guides and they are spaced in such a way as to distribute the strain uniformly over the blank.

Wrapping the guides

The rod guides should now be wrapped tight at the positions we have established. This is not particularly difficult, but it does require precision. This is the stage that mainly decides the finish of the rod.

The only way of wrapping a rod efficiently is with it lying horizontally in front of you in some form of "cradle", so that you have both hands free when necessary. How to make a wrapping rack from a pair of book ends was described in the chapter on tools. A holder for the rod wrapping thread is also needed, and it should stand on the surface of the worktable on the other side of the blank from where you are wrapping. Some instructions in rod crafting recommend that you use a thread holder for fly whipping, which hangs straight down from the blank. If you work like this you will have poor control over how the thread is wrapped round the rod, and you will also have to hold the thread holder with one hand while actually wrapping so that you will only have one hand left over to hold the blank. This makes the wrapping work both slow and tiring.

Fix instead the thread holder upright on a slab of wood, which is clamped to the opposite edge of the worktable, or pull the thread between the pages of a book placed on the table. The friction to the pages of the book tensions the thread, and this can be regulated by laying several books on top of each other. The reel of thread can be placed in a coffee cup on the other side of the pile of books. Ready-made thread holders can be purchased, or you can make one yourself from a slab of wood, the tip of a rod, a few pins for the thread rollers and a thread tensioner from an old sewing machine, although the method described above functions perfectly.

The wrapping is done by turning the blank towards you so that the thread is laid on its topside, which allows you to see how the thread in being laid and have full control of the result. Apart from a wrapping rack and thread tensioner you also need good lighting, a sharp hobby knife (preferably a razor blank or a scalpel), masking tape, and a tool to adjust and smooth the thread with – a crochet needle functions well.

Workplace for rod wrapping. You can work best if the rod is placed horizontally in a rack. Two modified bookends function well. The thread is placed in a glass and is tensioned by pulling it through the pages of a telephone directory. An additional directory on top of the first one increases the tension of the thread.

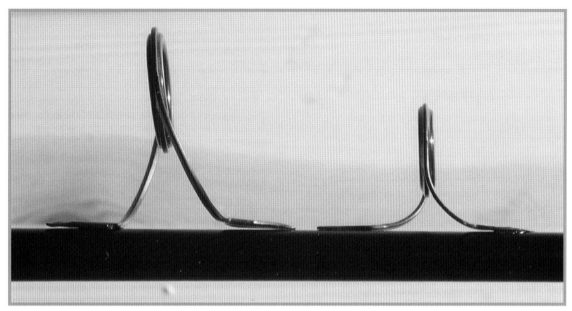

Preparation of the rod guide feet before they are wrapped on the rod. The left rod guide is skew and one foot is on its heel, which makes it impossible to wrap the thread up on it. The other is on its toe, which means that it will be pressed down into the blank material when wrapped. The right rod guide is upright and its feet are flush with the blank. The right foot of the guide is filed down for the wrap.

Preparing the rod guides

The guides may need a certain adjustment before they are wrapped tight on the rod. The outer ends of the guide feet are often quite thick, with a pronounced edge that has to be filed down. For the thread to climb up on the guide foot without problem when wrapping it should slope uniformly and finely until it merges with the surface of the blank. File the top of the guide foot with a fine-toothed file until it slopes gently down to the end that is to be thin, but not sharp.

File also the underside of the guide foot. Some guides have a pressed in honeycomb pattern to "grip" the blank. It is doubtful if this achieves the intended purpose, and above all it means that the outer end of the guide foot cannot lie flush with blank. In other words the pattern must be removed, at least in the outer end. Even guides without these patterns often have irregularities on the underside. Finally, use emery paper to smooth any burrs and sharp edges resulting from the filing. A razor-sharp edge can work its way into the blank and cause the rod to break.

The feet on two-footed guides are seldom completely in line with other. Carefully check that both feet are level on the blank. Guide feet that, so to speak, are "standing on their toes" can chaff down into the blank when the rod is working, which can lead to the rod breaking. If the guide is standing on its "heels" it will be impossible to wind the thread up on the guide foot. Adjust the guide feet with a pair of pliers until

both their undersides are flush with the blank. Carefully straighten angled guides with the pliers and check the adjustment of the guide feet one last time.

Wrapping techniques

Each wrap starts on the blank a short distance from the end of the guide foot. This first piece of the wrap outside the guide foot – the inset – has the main purpose of fastening the thread, and can be very short. The guide is held temporarily in place with a strip of tape, latex hose or O-ring, which is removed as soon as the thread covers enough of the guide foot to hold it firmly. The end of the guide foot must of course not be covered by tape.

Fasten the thread as follows. First wind a few loose turns with the end of the thread round the blank, so that the thread from the thread holder reaches the blank where the inset is to begin. The turns of thread are wound round over the blank towards you, down and under it and up on its opposite side to you. They should form a loose spiral from the starting point of the inset and in over the guide foot, in other words in the direction you are going to wrap. This is so that you will have something to hold when you are fastening the wrapping. The thread spiral should now be fastened to the blank by wrapping it over it where the inset begins.

Hold the end of the thread to the blank with your thumb,

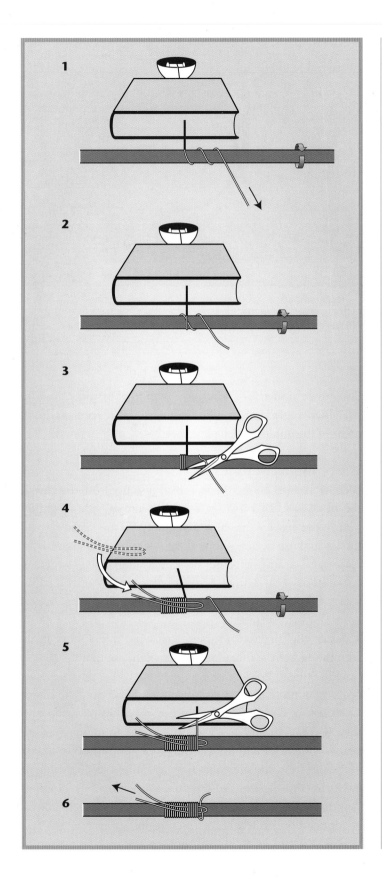

or fix it there with a small piece of tape. The first wrap should cross over the thread spiral/end exactly where the inset is to begin and press it against the blank. The next wrap is placed beside the first and crosses over and further presses the end to the blank. After another three to four tight wraps the thread will sit firmly and you can release your thumb. Cut off the end of the thread so that only a short stub sticks out and then wind turn after turn beside each other so that they cover the stub, and then go up onto the guide foot.

What can happen is that the thread wraps can end up too loose or too tight, on top of each other. In this case you will just have to go back, unwind the thread that has come wrong and do the wrapping again. The wraps should lie close to each other, but without being packed. Avoid pressing the thread together afterwards, since this will only produce irregularities and make it even more difficult to achieve a smooth wrap. Find instead the right angle between the thread and blank, which means that the wraps are correctly positioned straight away. After experimenting a little you will find it – close to but not exactly 90 degrees – so that the new turns are pressed beside those already wound. Take extra care on the upward slope on the guide foot. The thread will want to pack itself tighter there since the guide foot slopes upwards and the thread tension will automatically pull together the turns. One or two minor gaps is not a catastrophe – it will smooth out later – but there should not be any big gaps in the wrapping.

When 8 – 10 turns remain it is time to prepare the finish. Stick a loose thread end under the last wound turn so that it forms an eye, pointing in the direction the thread has been wound. Finish wrapping and cut off, pressing the thread with your thumb to the blank on the last turn. The thread end is now inserted through the thread eye and can be drawn in under the last turn, which will hold it secure with all its pressure.

The thread end will now stick out from the wrapping and

Fluff and frayed thread ends are burned off by moving the flame quickly over the wrap.

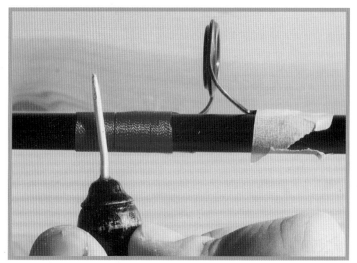

The finished wrap is rubbed in the lengthwise direction of the blank so that the threads will be evened out and fill up any gaps. The rubbing tool is the tip of a knitting needle fitted in a small wooden handle.

must be cut off so that it is completely concealed under the wrapping, which is a critical stage. In other words you have to cut it off just beside the wrapping but without cutting the threads. Everyone finds their own method and there are probably as many methods as there are rod crafters. Mine looks like this. Hold the thread end tensioned with one hand and follow it down between the turns of thread with the cutting edge of the knife. The knife should be held so that it cuts against the rod blank, straight down between the turns of thread. Carefully rub the knife against the blank – do not saw – and the thread end will be cut off and nothing else. The knife must be very sharp, and a razor blade is ideal.

Burning off, rubbing and lining up

There must be no fluff whatsoever from the ends of the thread on the wrapping, since this will produce annoying irregularities in the finish. If, however, there are small strands of thread sticking out you burn them off. Use preferably a spirit burner with wick, in emergencies a cigarette lighter can be used, but you have to be very careful because of the soot! Singe off the protruding fibers by quickly passing them over the flame.

Small gaps in the wrapping can be rubbed out – the rubbing flattens and spreads the threads, while smoothing out and moving the turns slightly. By rubbing in a certain direction you can move the thread so that it covers and fills out larger gaps. To do this you can use any sort of soft rounded

and polished small metal rod – knitting needle or crochet needle. The soft polished back end of a pair of tweezers or scalpel also works. Carefully rub the wrapping along the blank, from both ends of the wrapping and in to the middle, until the threads lie smoothly and tightly all over.

When all the guides are wrapped they have to be lined up. So far we have not been very precise, but the precision comes when you make the fine adjustments. Hold the blank vertically at arms length with the guide side turned away from you and close one eye. The guides that sit at an angle can be clearly seen and are carefully moved under the wrappings until they sit right. Make this adjustment by pressing on the side of the guide foot with your thumb. Avoid bending the guide keeper, since this can cause the guide to bend or press the guide foot down in the blank. When all the guides are lined up take careful aim through the guides and check that they form a straight line to the top ring.

Dust and chaff from the thread can be removed with a tackcloth. As soon as the wrapping is ready it is coated with color preserver.

Edging and other effects

Edging of the guide wraps and other effects are used to give the rod a personal appearance. If you coordinate the colors of the wraps with the color scales in the grip, blank, reel seat and rod guides, you will achieve a professional and attractive rod.

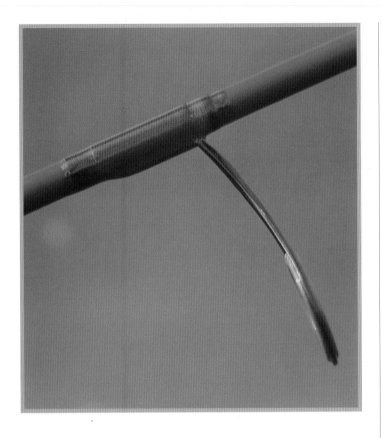

Below (left, centre & right): There are several ways of edging a wrap, and here is one. Wrap in two extra eyes when the wrap is started. When the main wrap is ready one of them is used to fasten the edge thread (illustration a). The edge thread is wrapped two-three turns and then finished with the second eye (illustration b). Illustration c shows the finished result.

The simplest way of edging a wrap is to wrap in two extra "finishing eyes" in the end of the wrap you want to have a decorative edge. When the main wrap is ready you first use one of the extra eyes to fasten the thread you are going to use for the decoration. Pull in the effect thread with the eye under the wrap so that it is locked in place. Wrap the effect thread round a few turns, after which the second of the extra eyes fastens the edging. With this method you can make very narrow edge rings.

Inserted threads in contrasting colors are striking and can be placed anywhere in the wrap. Cut off a stub of the thread to be inserted and stick it in under the main wrap. 8-10 turns more of the main wrap will fasten the effect thread. Now wrap the effect thread a few turns, 3-4 usually produce an interesting result. Continue as usual with the main wrap and wind over the end of the effect thread so that it is fixed. Another alternative is wind effect thread and the main thread together, or in other words both threads are wound beside each other at the same time. Fix the effect thread in the same way. Several threads of different colors wound beside each other often produce exciting results, and with a little practice you can wind a large number of threads at the same time.

Changing the color of the threads is done in the same way as when you start an edging. Wind in an eye in the wrap, stick the end of the thread you are changing to in the eye, and pull in and lock it under the finished part of the wrap. Cut off the old thread and lock its end with the new when you continue wrapping. When you change color you can do this by wrap-

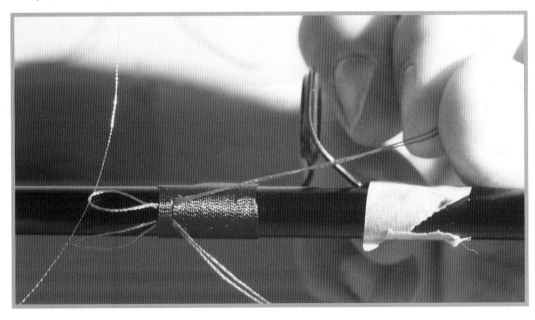

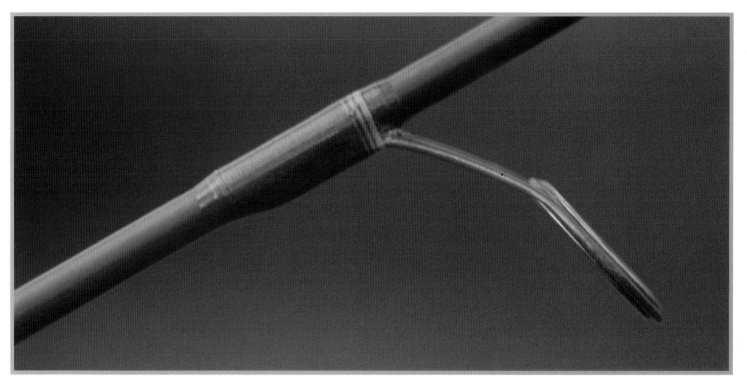

Edge effects can be made in many different ways. Here the yellow edge thread has been fastened before the main wrap was finished and the two threads have been wrapped together a little before the main thread was fastened and the edging finished.

ping the old and the new thread colors together for a short distance as described above, before you fasten the old thread and continue wrapping with the new. In this way you can achieve "toned" or "shadowed" effects. A series of color changes in this way that successively change from one color to another through several intermediate shades can produce an impression of being painted "wet on wet" or sprayed on the blank.

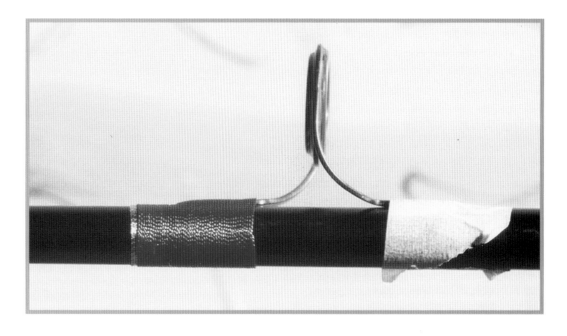

Different effects that can be used on guide wraps.

Under wraps

An under wrap is a wrap that is placed on the blank under the guide foot. The guide is then wrapped with an additional wrap over the first – the complete wrap in other words consists of two layers of thread, one that lies between the guide foot and blank, and one that holds the guide in place. Under wraps protect the blank from chaffing by the guide foot, while also holding the guide more securely. Under wraps in a different color provide automatic edgings, but they also increase the durability of the rod in several different ways.

One possible disadvantage is that the extra layer of thread absorbs lacquer and therefore increases the rod's inherent mass. The difference, however, is very slight and most blanks have no problem carrying the extra mass. It is more important how thickly the wraps are coated, and double wrapped rods with a thin layer of lacquer may very well have lighter wraps than single wrapped rods with thick beads of lacquer on each wrap. It is preferable to use under wraps on all rods, possibly with the exception of the very lightest.

The difficulty is that the upper wrap, i.e. the second layer of thread, often wants to creep down between the under wrap, which emphasizes all the irregularities and cannot be smoothed when the wrapping is ready. The solution is a very smooth under wrap and to wind the upper wrap with slightly less tension than the under wrap. If you wrap the upper wrap in the opposite direction to the under wrap, or with slightly thicker thread, then the under wrap will not be able to steer the thread in the upper wrap.

There is another way of securing the guide feet, and this should be used on one-footed guides. When the wrapping has come to the point where the guide keeper lifts up from the guide foot – where you normally finish off – you continue the wrapping a few extra turns instead past the guide keeper down on the blank. These last turns form, when they are coated, a "heel" in the end of the wrap and prevent the guide foot from gliding out from the wrap.

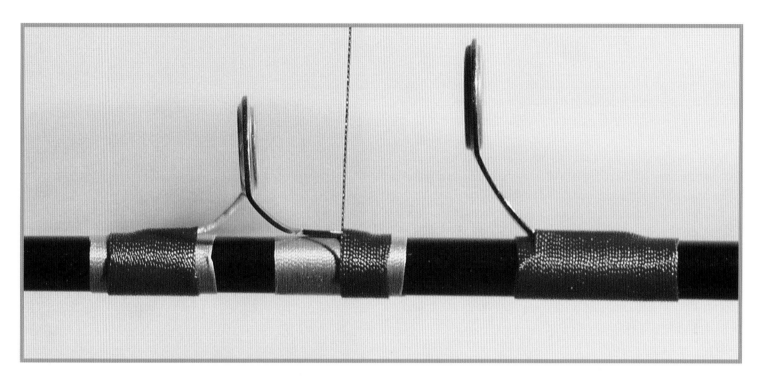

Above: Different effects that can be used on guide wraps. Under-wrap. The rod guide to the left is wrapped with the under-wrap, which protects the blank and holds the guide more securely. The right guide is secured in that the wrap is continued a few turns down on the blank, after the guide foot is covered, so that the thread forms a heel and prevents the guide from sliding out from the wrap.

Below: Apart from holding the guide more securely an under-wrap is decorative. Natural edgings are formed. The effect to the right before the end of the wrap is achieved by wrapping the brown upper thread thinly on the lower thread a little.

Decorative wraps

"Butt wraps" are decorative wraps that cover 15-20 centimeters of the blank above the grip, a decoration that is sometimes strongly questioned by rod crafters. Many of them mean that a rod should be built as spartanly as possible and that nothing that does not have some function belongs on it. This is naturally a matter of taste and fancy, but also of "good taste" – a rod with exaggerated decorations of the most glittering and garish type obviously produces a cheap and tasteless impression.

My opinion is that a rod should have an exclusive appearance. A Custom rod, which is what this is about, should also explain through its appearance that it is something out of the ordinary. A tastefully composed and discrete butt wrap with a range of colors that merge into the rest of the rod is a way of accentuating the exclusivity of the rod that ought to appeal even to the most conservative.

The final look of a Custom rod is unfortunately often given far too much attention, as if beautiful wraps and wooden parts were the only thing that distinguish it from a "standard rod". It would be a pity if an exaggerated emphasis on cosmetic aspects, which a butt wrap naturally is, prevented focusing on the real qualities of a rod. Since the very idea of Custom crafting is functional adjustment and maximum quality, one ought instead to pay attention to the rod's function and performance.

However, what we are really talking about is how to actually wrap butt wraps. The basic technique is rather simple. Wind a thread in a spiral up and down the blank so that it crosses itself at several points in a row, a row with crosses on the topside of the rod and another opposite, on the underside. If the distance between two crosses in the same row is equally long as the circumference of the blank you will get a 90 degree angle between the threads in the cross. Build up the sides by wrapping several threads in different colors beside the first, so that a pattern is built up. That was all, now everybody can wrap butt wraps …

In practice a little more than this is needed of course. Careful planning of how the wrap is to sit, the layout, is one of the prerequisites for an attractive decorative wrap. Without planning the pattern will often come skew and uneven, which is never attractive and usually ends up with you having to redo a lot of work. Start by marking how close to the grip the pattern is to begin. Not precisely up against the grip since there must be space to finish off at both ends of the decora-

tive wrap. Draw a ring round the blank with a pencil where the pattern is to begin, at least a few centimeters from the top end of the grip, and further up if the blank is a thick one. Another way is to very carefully scratch with a needle in lacquered surface of the blank, without going down to the fibers underneath. Do not use this method on blanks of high-module graphite or with a matt surface.

Toned, short butt wraps.

Now draw a line along the blank exactly opposite it on its topside, i.e. so that the line lies exactly opposite the side of the rod you can see when holding it in front of you when fishing, and another line exactly opposite on the underside of the rod. It is only on these lines that the crosses should lie.

Now mark the position of the crosses along the two lines so that all the crosses have a relatively equal spacing. The first cross on the underside of the blank should lie exactly on the line that marks the upper limit of the wrapping. The crosses on the underside of the blank should be displaced a half space in relation to the upper crosses, so that every other cross is on the topside and every other on the underside, with regular intervals all the way. If you position the marks in this way it will be possible to wrap a thread in an even spiral round the blank so that the thread crosses both the layout lines opposite each cross mark. Mark the number of crosses required and then where the wrapping should end, once again so that the edge of the wrap comes opposite one of the crosses on the underside. Draw a new line round the complete blank there.

Now place a piece of double-adhesive tape round the blank just over the upper end mark – space for the finish – and another piece round the upper end of the grip, i.e. a piece below the wrap's lower end mark – once again space for the finish. The purpose of the tape is to hold all the threads in position during the work until the wrapping is ready. The distance between the wrap's edge marking and the tape should be the at least the same as the distance between two crosses on the same line. Protect the blank and grip with a few turns of standard masking tape before the double-adhesive tape is put

Below: The layout thread is first wound in a spiral in one direction, and then back, so that it crosses itself several times. These crosses are spread out at regular intervals in two straight lines, one on each side of the blank.

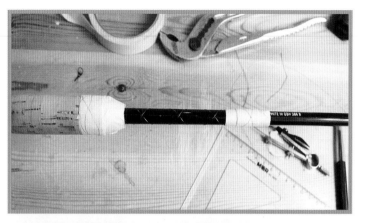

These two series of photos show how it is possible to build up two different types of patterns from the layout. Left column: the original layout cross of gold thread is built up with threads only on the right side, seen from the observer. The thread color alternates successively from black over brown to beige, after which the pattern is edged with gold and brown again. An angular shaped pattern with the point to the right in the illustration is created.

In the right column the pattern is built out on all sides. The color goes from black over brown, wine-red, red and orange to beige again. Finally the pattern is edged on the left side in the illustration and filled out completely. A prism or a rhomb is built up.

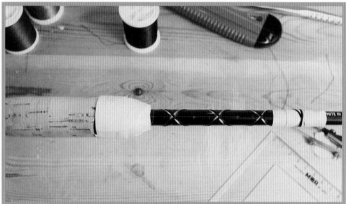

on. This makes it easier to remove it all when you are finished, and once you have started with the butt wrapping the tension in the thread can get to be quite considerable so that without such a protective layer the thread can cut into the grip cork and leave permanent marks.

Precision is important when the first thread is wrapped – the layout thread. The layout thread will govern all of the subsequent pattern, and if the wrapping is to be even it must come exactly opposite all the marks. Start by fixing the thread in the grip by wrapping a few turns round the double-adhesive tape and then wrap in a spiral up the blank, making sure to lay it exactly opposite each cross mark. When the thread is up at the upper double-adhesive tape it is wound few turns round this to fix it properly, after which you wind it back down to the grip again, exactly opposite each mark. Finish off with a few turns round the double-adhesive tape again to fasten it, and cut the thread.

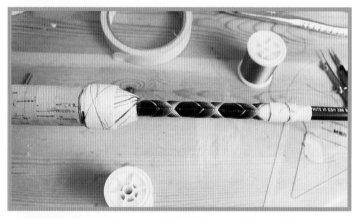

The rod is in other words rotating in the same direction when you are wrapping. First you wrap up, and then you wrap down, while the downward going thread crosses the one that is wrapped upwards and opposite each cross mark. When the thread is secured at the bottom again, adjust in all the crosses exactly on the marks. You can move the thread by carefully pressing it to the side with a knitting needle or a crochet needle. Make sure that no sharp metal objects are pressed into the material in the blank. Ready! The rest of the wrapping is easy.

Wrap another thread on each side of the layout thread, in other words there will be three threads going up and down the blank, with the layout thread in the middle. A small rhomb-like shape, the beginning of a prism, will be formed where the three threads cross each other. Continue building the prism with new threads on all sides. When it is large enough you go over to another thread color, and continue building up with different threads in a combination of colors

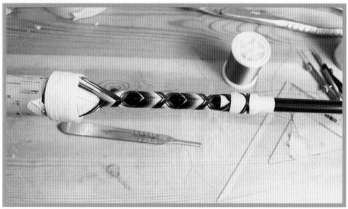

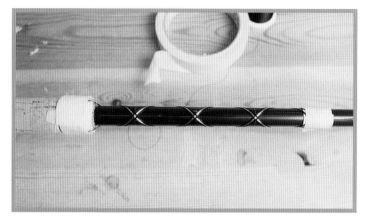

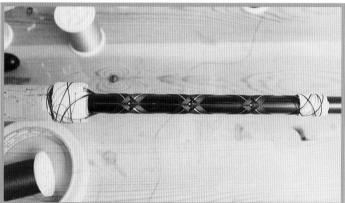

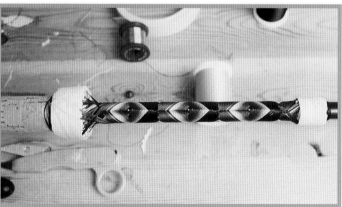

that appeals to you. If you experiment a little you will soon find out which color combinations are suitable.

Different patterns

The principles for building up different forms of patterns are briefly as follows. If as above you wrap thread on both sides of the layout thread so that the cross points are built up in all directions a prism pattern is formed. If instead you wrap only on one side of the layout thread the cross points will only be built out in one direction. A V-shaped pattern is built up, and depending on which side of the pattern you place the thread you can direct the V-pattern in different directions. You can change the direction of the V-pattern by changing the side of the layout thread you build the pattern on, and you can also change between prism shapes and V-shapes in the same wrap.

By wrapping with two different thread colors on each side of the layout thread the prism can be divided up into halves or quarters with triangular form. By changing these colors backwards and forwards you can also achieve different effects. If for example all the threads lying under the layout thread, i.e. on the grip side of this, are blue, and all of them lying over these, i.e. up on the rod, are red, the rhomb will be divided horizontally into two halves, the lower blue and the upper red.

You can build out a prism or a V-shape more to one side than the other. You do this by placing one thread for every turn on one side of the layout thread, and two or more threads on the other.

Another variant is to successively increase the number of threads per turn on one side of a prism, while you keep it constant on the other. The above mentioned pattern with one lower and one upper half in different colors can be developed in this way. Increase, for example, with one thread per turn on one side, while the lower side is wrapped with one thread per turn. In other words you wrap a blue thread on the layout thread's lower side, up and back down. A red thread is then wrapped on the layout thread's upper side, also up and then down, followed by a blue on the underside again and now two red on the upper side. There will then be, alternating from underside to topside: one blue under, three red over, one blue under, four red over, etc. The result will be that the border between the two colors in each prism will be curved, so that its edges curve off upwards on the rod.

Changing the thread colors with toned effects is achieved in the same way as in ring wraps. Very interesting results are

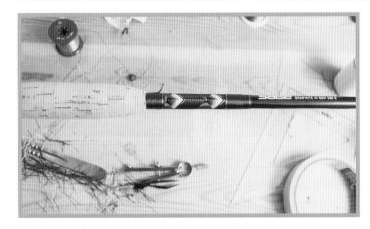

The illustrations show the finished result.

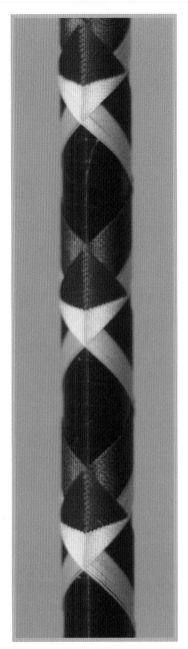

obtained by switching from one color to another successively, by reducing the number of threads of the first color step by step and mixing in more and more of the other. You can, for example, go over from brown to yellow by first mixing in a yellow thread and then adding three brown threads, and then two yellow, two brown, three yellow, one brown, and finally pure yellow. If you also allow the transition to go from brown over red-orange to yellow in the same way the toning will become even smoother.

Combinations are used to build up more advanced patterns. For example, you can start by laying out two or more layout threads a short distance from each other so that they form pairs or groups of crosses with the same relative distance between the groups. The crosses in one pair or one group can be placed a few millimeters or more from each other, which is regulated by the distance between the different layout threads. By building up the different crosses in the groups in different ways, in different directions and with different colors, you can

Above left: Color divided prism. The division has been achieved in that all the threads wound below the layout thread, as seen in the illustration, were beige, while those above were wine-red. Each "turn" consists of first a beige thread on one side of the layout threads, followed by two wine-red on the other side, which has produced the angle of the border between the colors.

Above right: The border between the wine-red and the blue color in this prism curves in an arc. This has been achieved in that the number of wine-red threads were increased by one for each "turn". First a blue thread on one side of the layout threads, and a wine-red on the other side of them, followed by a blue and two wine-red, and blue and three wine-red, and so on. The wrap is finished with a band of four beige threads on the left side of the prism.

With combinations of layout crosses built up in different directions and at different rates it is possible to achieve a large number of effects. You can provide the butt wrap with birds and butterflies, achieve three-dimensional effects, and even wrap a row of fish on your rod.

imitate birds, fish, butterflies, flowers, medallions, crosses and a lot more. The only limits are set by your imagination.

A soon as the wrapping has a tendency to thin out you pack the threads together against the layout threads by means of a knitting needle, after which you rub the wrap smooth. The rubbing also spreads out the threads and gets them to cover the thin parts. At intervals you renew the double-adhesive tape. New tape is placed over the old and in this way secures all the previous wraps.

If you want to have all the blank covered with decorative wraps you just continue widening the pattern until the threads that lie round one cross meet the ones lying round the next. This requires a very careful layout! If the distance between the crosses is not exactly the same everywhere there will be different distances between the turns of the layout thread when it goes in a spiral up and down the blank. This can cause the pattern to "grow together" at one point, while there are still large gaps in it at others. If you cannot manage

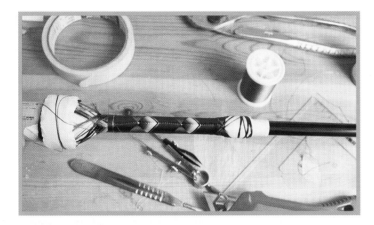

Top: Finishing off a butt wrap. Start by wrapping over all the threads, from the bottom end of the pattern out to the tape that holds it all at the grip.

Center: When the wrap holds the thread in the butt wrap all the threads are cut at the tape. Remove all the tape and comb out the thread ends.

Bottom: All the threads are shortened and frayed up, so that the fixing thread can be wrapped over them and down onto the blank with an imperceptible transition.

to pack the threads together enough where the pattern goes together to make space for a sufficient number of extra threads, then it will be impossible to get the pattern to go together in the thin end without the thread starting to climb up onto each other in the tight end. In which case you will just have to start again, which is not much fun since this sort of wrapping takes a few hours to wrap.

The wrapping is finished and secured at both ends with a normal wrap that covers and holds the ends of the pattern threads. Start this anchor wrap in the middle of the marking made earlier for the edge of the pattern, i.e. in the middle of the cross on the underside of the blank which came opposite the middle of the pattern's edge marking. Wrap outwards in the direction of the double-adhesive tape, and with quite high-tensioned thread.

When the wrap is just over one centimeter wide you can cut off all the thread ends from the double-adhesive tape and remove it. Use the knife carefully and pay attention to the thread tension! If you should cut off the wrong thread, or if the thread tension is released in this stage, you will be left with a few loose threads instead of a butt wrap.

"Comb out" all crossing, cut thread ends, and shorten them until they can be completely covered by thread by continuing with the anchor wrap a few more centimeters. Fray up and thin out the thread ends by scraping them with the back of the knife out towards the ends. This thins out the bundle of threads that is to be wrapped over at the end, so that the transition to the blank can by made neatly and smoothly.

Remove dust and frayed threads by pressing the sticky side of a strip of tape against the frayed thread ends and then finally wrapping over them until all the thread ends are covered. Finish off, remove all the tape and immediately apply color preserver to secure the wrap.

Lacquering and finish

Your rod is almost finished, all that is needed is the lacquer to protect the wraps from wear and then you can take your creation to your favorite fishing spots and enjoy the reward of your labors. But one detail does actually remain. The result – the handcrafted rod – is a personal combination of technology and crafting, and like all artists you should naturally sign your work.

The best tool to write neatly with on a rod blank is a hand lettering pen of the old fashioned type dipped in a inkpot. They can be bought as loose nibs and wooden holders. Both nibs and holders can be found in a well-sorted bookshop or in a shop for artists' materials. Chose a nib with the thinnest tip possible.

Water-based, white ink can be bought at the same place, otherwise white water-based hobby paint can be diluted with water until it is thin enough to write with. Test by writing with the ink on a bright surface, leave to dry, and apply a little rod lacquer to make sure that the ink is not dissolved when you lacquer the rod.

If the ink will not adhere you can carefully rub the bright surface of the blank with fine steel wool. This should not be done, and neither is it necessary, on blanks with a matt surface. Practice the lettering on a broken rod, or the like, until you can write your name and the date neatly. It takes a little practice on a round surface. Sign the rod and allow the ink to dry. Do not cover the inscription with color preserver, since both ink and hobby paint are soluble in water and there is a risk that the water-based color preserver will dissolve the ink.

All wraps should be treated with color preserver, it is needed to preserve the color of the thread, shrink it, and to fill the spaces in the wrap so that bubbles of air are not formed in the lacquer. Do not apply rod lacquer directly on the wraps, but use primer first. Water-based color preserver is used for polymer and epoxy lacquers. First drench the wrap with one lot, diluted with 50 % water, and leave to dry. Now apply two ample lots of full strength so that all the spaces are filled up. Allow to dry well between the lots because if new color preserver is applied on something that is not dry it will become milky. A channel is formed on both sides of each ring foot at

Propelling pencil on holder and white ink for signing.

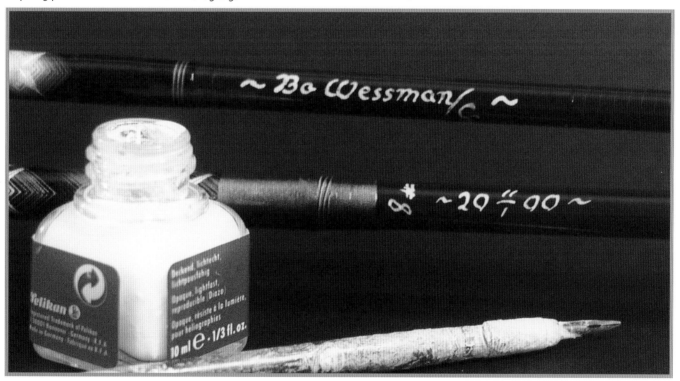

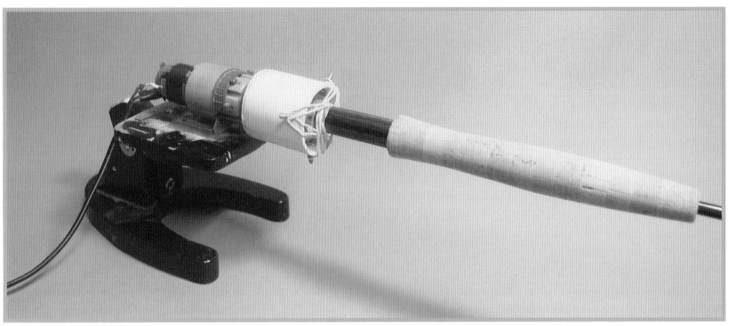

My old lacquer curing device consists of an electric model motor on a microscope stand. The plastic tube is fixed on the motor shaft, into which the rod is inserted and held in position by rubber bands placed on the three pins in the edge of the tube. The motor is driven by a transformer and the speed is regulated with a rheostat.

an angle between the ring foot, thread and blank. It is important that this space is fully filled, because if there is any air left here there will be bubbles in the final coat.

Two-component polymer and epoxy lacquers produce bright, transparent surfaces and never turn yellow with age. Mix the base and hardener according to the instructions in a dust free container. I used disposable muffin forms of paper or aluminum, but make sure they are not pretreated with cooking fat, some forms are. Mix well, but slowly to avoid mixing in air. Air bubbles cause irregularities in the finished lacquer, which have to be removed. Because of the viscosity of the lacquer it takes a while for all the air bubbles to rise and during this time the lacquer begins to cure, which can cause problems when it is to be applied on the last wraps. Large bubbles rise more quickly than small ones, so it is a good idea if you can both avoid stirring down bubbles into the lacquer and breaking up those that form to even smaller bubbles. Allow the lacquer to stand for a while in a wide, shallow container, e.g. a muffin form, and meanwhile remove any dust from the rod with a tackcloth. When all the air has risen to the surface you can blow lightly into the container to burst all the bubbles.

Applying the lacquer

The brush should be soft and it is easiest to brush out the rather high-viscous lacquer thinly if it has short bristles. Apply the lacquer evenly and brush out as thinly as possible without forming uneven patches. It is a question of striking a balance between too thick and too thin. This type of viscous lacquer is intended to produce a smooth glossy surface without the thread structure going through. Patches will form between the glossy sections if you brush it too thinly, where the structure of the thread will be seen in the surface of the lacquer. This produces an ugly uneven surface, and in this case more lacquer is needed

Start lacquering the rod at the top. The lacquer will begin to cure while you are working and it is easier to brush it out thinly on the thicker sections of the blank, so we can leave them to the last. Apply lacquer over all the wraps and over the inscription.

After applying the lacquer carefully check all the wraps – several times. Check for air bubbles. There can be air under the threads that only creeps out after quite a while, so during the first few hours after lacquering it is a good idea to go over the rod several times and look for bubbles. All bubbles that rise to the surface must be removed. You can remove them by carefully blowing on them, or by quickly scorching them with a spirit burner, in which case they usually burst. If this does not help you will have to burst them with a needle.

It can also happen, if you have applied the lacquer too thinly, that they creep away at certain places as described above so that you get uneven patches where the surface structure of the thread comes through. In this case you will have to apply more lacquer on the exposed area. This can be done during the first one to two hours. You quite simply place a drop of lacquer on the actual area so that it covers all the exposed thread, and when you rotate the rod during the drying the drop will spread out and form a uniform surface with the rest of the lacquer on the wrap.

The rod should rotate in a dustless area during the curing, otherwise the lacquer will run off or hang on the side facing down. Use an electric motor that gives approximately 4 revolutions a minute, fix the butt end of the rod to its shaft (since we have still not fixed on the butt cap it is easy to fix the rod on the shaft), and place it in the above described wrapping rack. Protect the surface of the blank with masking tape where is rests against the recesses in the rack.

Battery operated grill motors can be purchased in hardware shops, and they are not very expensive. If you cannot get hold of a rotation motor you can also place the rod in the wrapping rack and turn it at regular internals until the lacquer has stopped running, which takes 3-4 hours.

Your rod is now ready.

If you follow these instructions this should result in a rod that will bring you great satisfaction and pleasure during many, many hours of fishing. It will also have all the prerequisites to surpass anything that can be bought ready-made – even if it is your first rod. An important part of the satisfaction that it can give, is of course the fact that you have made it yourself.

But the rod will actually also make you more successful as a fisherman. It is a known fact that the fisherman who believes in what he is doing fishes better, since he fishes more perseveringly, more attentively and more creatively. And it is important for this belief to know that the tackle functions as it should and that you can use it to the full. The person who has crafted his own rod has an instrument that is directly adapted to his very self and what he does, and the quality and characteristics of which he has one hundred percent control over. You could hardly wish for better prerequisites than this.

Index